Earthkeepers

Earth-keepers

Environmental Perspectives on Hunger, Poverty, and Injustice

Art & Jocele Meyer

Foreword by Calvin B. DeWitt

HERALD PRESS
Scottdale, Pennsylvania
Waterloo, Ontario

Library of Congress Cataloging-in-Publication Data
Meyer, Art, 1928-
   Earthkeepers : environmental perspectives on hunger, poverty, and injustice / Art and Jocele Meyer.
     p. cm.
   Includes bibliographical references.
   ISBN 0-8361-3544-X (alk. paper)
   1. Human ecology—Religious aspects—Christianity. 2. Human ecology—Moral and ethical aspects. 3. Pollution. 4. Environmental policy. I. Meyer, Jocele, 1928-   II. Title. III. Title : Earthkeepers.
GF80.M48 1991
304.2—dc20   90-24473
                                                   CIP

The paper used in this publication is recycled and meets the minimum requirements of American National Standard for Information Sciences— Permanence of Paper for Printed Library Materials, ANSI Z39.48-1984.

Unless otherwise indicated, Scripture quotations are from *The Holy Bible: New International Version*, copyright © 1973, 1978, 1984 by the International Bible Society; used by permission of Zondervan Bible Publishers. Other quotations used by permission are marked RSV, from the Revised Standard Version of the Bible, copyright 1946, 1952, 1971 by the Division of Christian Education of the National Council of the Churches of Christ in the USA; KJV, from the King James Version of *The Holy Bible*; NEB, from *The New English Bible*, copyright © by the Delegates of the Oxford University Press and the Syndics of the Cambridge University Press 1961, 1970; NRSV, from *The New Revised Standard Version Bible*, copyright © 1989 by the Division of Christian Education of the National Council of the Churches of Christ in the USA; TEV, from *Today's English Version*, or the *Good News Bible*, Old Testament copyright © by the American Bible Society in 1976, and New Testament copyright © by the American Bible Society in 1966, 1971, 1976.

99 98 97 96 95 94 93 92 91 10 9 8 7 6 5 4 3 2 1

To our children and our grandchildren
who must take the initiative
to be good earthkeepers
in the coming generations

Contents

PART FOUR: Food and Energy

PART FIVE: Sustainable Agriculture

Foreword

"I dream that the Christian church, with its many dedicated members, will take up the challenge and become an instrument of change. In that role, the church as God's people will courageously be a prophetic voice in a world that has lost its course." This is the message and hope of this book—written at a time when Earth and its creatures have come to a severe crisis of degradation under heavy human exploitation and abuse. It is a hope that looks forward to something: toward the coming of the children of God— toward the coming of Earth's keepers.

Art and Jocele Meyer, in this compelling book, identify as part of the human problem our misunderstanding of how the natural world really works—and our violation of creation's laws and limits. They rightly advocate that "we must learn to live within the limitations of God's created order, conserving, using renewable resources, and recycling natural resources." We must follow the example of Jesus, who understood that all creatures in God's creation are related. Hence he "lived lightly on the Earth and warned his disciples against hoarding material possessions and allowing their heart to be enticed by the lure of wealth and power."

Beginning with a prayer of thanksgiving and confession, and building from biblical principles derived from both the Old and the New Testaments, the authors delve deeply into the causes of Earth's degradation. Their probing finds that current economic systems arrogantly neglect the principles by which creation operates. These systems assume (1) we can be independent from nature, (2) we can throw our wastes "away," (3) we can improve upon nature's systems and fix any "problem" nature presents, and (4) we can get more out of a system than we put into it.

But, the authors show, these assumptions violate ecological principles. This gives us no recourse but to reorder our economic systems in accord with the way creation is ordered. And Meyers find that the biblical design is one that provides an answer since it is compatible with ecological laws.

The biblical design of faith and economics, the writers maintain, calls for conserving energy and developing alternative renewable forms of it, stabilizing the human population, recycling all materials, protecting and renewing the environment, and developing lifestyles that incorporate these actions. God's economy, in contrast to our present economy, is one which (1) recognizes ourselves as creatures in creation, (2) is a recycling economy, (3) is good and not in need of improvement, and (4) recognizes that we never get more out of a natural system than what is put into it. Our economy, modeled after God's economy, should be dependable, regenerative, sustainable, and thoroughly consistent with the laws by which creation is ordered. This is part of *Earthkeepers'* prophetic voice. But there is more.

The Meyers' probing finds that peacemaking must now quite consciously embrace *all* of creation. There can be no peace in a degraded creation. Degraded environment brings poverty, hunger, injustice, and war. And war and preparations for war powerfully degrade the environment. Thus, "to work at achieving a healthy environment is to work at significant peacemaking in today's world." We are moved to accept the writers' conclusion: "It is the responsibility of Christians through the church and otherwise to work toward the elimination of both war and environmental degradation. The vicious cycle of war leading to environmental degradation and vice versa must be broken if the creation is to be preserved, maintained, and protected." And the church is crucially important to bring the needed changes; it appears to be about the only institution with the necessary ethical power.

Thus, this book brings environmental concern and action as a central focus of the church. It convinces us that addressing creation's degradation is much more than another cause to consider supporting. It moves us to see the problem and its Christian solution not only as *crucial* for the world but *vital* for the church and the kingdom of God. The mission of the church in creation is illustrated by the authors in their quoting a Philippine pastoral letter: "As people of the covenant we are called to protect endangered ecosystems like our forests, mangroves, and coral reefs and to establish just human communities in our land. More and more we must recognize that the commitment to work for justice and to preserve the integrity of creation are two inseparable dimensions of our Christian vocation to work for the kingdom of God in our times."

The Meyers reinforce this statement by personal experience in Haiti. There they identify devastating destruction of the natural environment as the cause of political repression and economic poverty. Haiti is viewed as a microcosm of an overpopulated, environmentally degraded Earth. Thus they demonstrate graphically what can (and will) happen where the economic powers that be, in collusion with political powers, mercilessly exploit land and people, taking the last traces of fruitfulness from the land.

Beyond war, economics, and politics, the Meyers probe deeper —looking into a future where human arrogance, ignorance, and greed are supported by misused biotechnology. Up until now, new forms have arisen only from the created order itself. This world now is a place where the hands and minds of people lead to human capabilities to create new life forms. The authors warn that the integrity of the created order is at stake.

This new ability to reorder creation in response to forces of the market and politics, the Meyers place before the church as a new and overwhelmingly important issue. The teachings of Genesis about human beings having chosen to abandon the garden by seeking to "do creation one better" are confirmed in our day by creation's degradation. The church and its members must now confront an ominous question: Will the market decide how creation will be ordered? Or will its *Earthkeepers*?

Already the market has converted much of our agriculture into agribusiness, and much of our Christian culture into worldly business. A crucial task of the church in addressing environmental and social degradation, is to reinstate the *culture* of land, family, home, and church. Needed is the restoration of culture with its foundation in biblical ethics.

This book begins appropriately with words of hope from Romans 8: "The creation waits in eager expectation for the sons of God to be revealed." Paulos Gregorios, whose translations of John and Colossians the Meyers cite, has also given a paraphrase of this passage in Romans: "The whole creation is groaning. . . ." "The creation waits—with neck outstretched, on tippy toes—for the coming of the children of God." The creation is waiting. . . .

As we begin to meet the challenge presented by this book, as individuals, families, and church—as we increasingly strive to be keepers of the Earth—we might well ask the following question: Will *we* satisfy creation's expectation? Are we worth creation's waiting? Will this eager creation—so earnestly looking for salvation through the children of God—be assured and fulfilled by *our* coming? The answer we *must* be able to give is clear. We must not let creation down. We must not forsake the one who never forsakes us. We must pray "Thy will be done!" And then we must do it!

Calvin B. DeWitt
Au Sable Institute of Environmental Studies
Oregon, Wisconsin

Authors' Preface

All is not well with the earth and its people. Never before has there been such a need to understand so many environmental problems and act on them.

In North America, evidence of environmental trouble is all around:

- Every community is looking for landfill space. Radioactive and other toxic wastes are building up. Medical waste, raw sewage, and garbage are washing up on East Coast beaches.
- Underground gasoline storage tanks in thousands of gas stations are rusting and leaking into water supplies. More and more drinking water is unfit to drink.
- Acid rain is affecting forests and lakes in many sections of North America.
- Consecutive summers of extreme heat and drought hint that a global warming trend, the greenhouse effect, may have arrived.
- Air pollution in United States (U.S.) cities is far beyond safe standards.
- The protective ozone layer in the earth's atmosphere is breaking down.
- Pesticides threaten thousands of farm workers and consumers.

Worldwide, improved communication and scientific record-keeping show global environmental problems:

- World population is increasing by 1.7 percent per year. At this rate, it will double in 40 years.
- Arable land continues to decrease by 36 million acres per year: 20 million by urbanization, 7 million by soil erosion, and 4.5 million by desertification and toxification.

The genetic diversity on which modern plant breeding depends is being undermined by habitat and species destruction.

Oil and gas (nonrenewable fossil fuels) are being rapidly depleted. Supplies could be exhausted within 50 to 75 years. Surface mining for coal and other natural resources damages land which often can never be properly restored.

It is our view that the problems of world hunger, poverty, conflict, and injustice are intricately intertwined with environmental issues. We have come to this perspective through study and observations in a number of countries as staff members in the Mennonite Central Committee U.S. Office of Development Education, now called the Office of Global Education under the MCC U.S. Peace Section. For the past seven years, we have written and spoken about hunger and ecology. This book arises out of some of our essays and discussions on these subjects.

Mennonite Central Committee (MCC) is the relief, service, and development agency of North American Mennonite and Brethren in Christ churches. Today there are over 1,000 workers in more than 50 countries.

We are convinced that there is a great need for the church to become more involved in the issues of hunger and ecology. The rationale for this is found in the first part of the book, where biblical-ethical foundations are discussed.

Defining and interpreting the major problems of environmental degradation is the subject of the second section of the book. Since energy—the vital ingredient for all of life—is interrelated with the environment, it is considered next. Following are sections on world population pressures, ecology, and economics; the relationship between environmental degradation and conflict; genetic engineering (biotechnology) and its relationship to world hunger and environment; and sustainable food and farm policy.

While the problems are immense and complex, we are optimistic. We talk about signs of hope in the epilogue. We are convinced that as the church becomes more involved and is willing to become a prophetic voice, these problems can be resolved.

We are indebted to many people for assistance in writing this book. Kristina Mast Burnett, head of information services at Mennonite Central Committee when we began this project, encouraged us to put some of our writing into book form. Charmayne Denlinger Brubaker, of the same MCC department, edited many of the articles later adapted for this book. A number of pieces first appeared in MCC News Service and in the MCC U.S. Global Education Office newsletter, *Food and Hunger Notes*.

Thanks to all manuscript editors and readers: Kenton Brubaker for comments on the general outline, Greg Bowman for content flow and sentence structure, Cynthia Nolt for content analysis, and Gordon Hunsberger for input from the Canadian viewpoint.

Sandy Weaver typed most of the original pieces while many MCC typists were involved later.

Our appreciation goes also to Calvin B. DeWitt, who graciously agreed to write the foreword.

Many others who knew about the writing of this book—family, friends, MCC colleagues—deserve thanks for their continuing encouragement.

Finally to S. David Garber, who edited the book at Herald Press, we express our deep appreciation.

We hope this book will stimulate you to better understand the problems discussed and to make appropriate responses.

Written largely out of our experience as educators in the United States, this volume may be used as a reader or as a study book. Following each main topic are discussion questions and a list of references. General resources are listed at the end of the book. We hope this book is used in Sunday school classes, special workshop sessions, and high school and college classrooms.

Art and Jocele Meyer

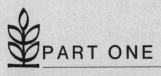

PART ONE

Stewardship of Creation— Earthkeeping

Biblical-Ethical Foundations

The creation waits in eager expectation for the sons of God to be revealed. For the creation was subjected to frustration, not by its own choice, but by the will of the one who subjected it, in hope that the creation itself will be liberated from its bondage to decay and brought into the glorious freedom of the children of God.
      —Romans 8:19-21

1. A Prayer of Thanksgiving and Confession

This prayer is from the official document of the first North American Conference on Christianity and Ecology held at Epworth Forest, North Webster, Indiana, August 1987:

For the marvelous grace of Your Creation—
We pour out our thanks to You, our God,
    for sun and moon and stars,
    for rain and dew and winds,
    for winter cold and summer heat.

We pour forth our praise to You
    for mountains and hills,
    for springs and valleys,
    for rivers and seas.

We praise You, O Lord,
    for plants growing in earth and water,
    for life inhabiting lakes and seas,
    for life creeping in soils and land,
    for creatures living in wetlands and waters,
    for life flying above earth and sea,
    for beasts dwelling in woods and fields.

How many and wonderful are Your works our God!
In wisdom You have made them all! (based on Psalm 147-8;
        104:24)

But we confess, dear Lord,
    as creatures privileged with the care and keeping of Your
        Creation,
    that we have abused Your Creation gifts
    through arrogance, ignorance, and greed.

We confess risking permanent damage to Your handiwork;
    we confess impoverishing Creation's ability to bring You
        praise.

Yet, we confess that Your handiwork displays Your glory,
    leaving all of us without excuse
    but to know You (based on Romans 1:20).
We confess that Your handiwork
    provides the context of our living;
    it is our home,
    it is the realm in which we live the life of Your kingdom:
    Your kingdom that is now in our midst and coming yet
        more fully.

We confess, Lord, that we often are unaware
    of how deeply we have hurt Your good earth
    and its marvelous gifts.

We confess that we often are unaware
    of how our abuse of Creation
    has also been an abuse of ourselves.

O Lord, how long will it take before we awaken to what we
        have done?
    How many waters must we pollute?
    How many woodlots must we destroy?
    How many forests must we despoil?
    How much soil must we erode and poison, O Lord?

How much of Earth's atmosphere must we contaminate?
How many species must we abuse and extinguish?
How many people must we degrade and kill with toxic
    wastes
  before we learn to love and respect Your Creation;
  before we learn to love and respect our home?

For our wrongs, Lord, we ask forgiveness.

In sorrow for what we have done
  we offer our repentance.
We pray that our actions toward You and Your Creation
  are worthy of our repentance;
    that we will so act here on earth
      that heaven will not be a shock to us.

May Thy kingdom come and Thy will be done on earth!

In our hearts, Lord, we promise anew
  to reverence Creation as a convicting witness
      of Your presence,
    eternal power, and
    divine majesty (based on Psalm 19 and Romans 1:20).

We promise to reverence Your Creation as a gracious gift
  entrusted to us by You, our God.
We promise anew to be stewards
  and not pillagers
  of what You have entrusted to us.

Indeed, we acknowledge
  that You have entrusted Your very Self to us
  in Creation, through your Incarnation in Christ Jesus.
For the Word through Whom all Creation was made
      and is upheld,
  that Word "became flesh and dwelt among us, . . .
  full of grace and truth" (John 1:14, RSV).

Lord, you pitched Your divine tent among us
and made our home Your home as well.

Creator God,
You have given us every reason
to learn and promote the wisdom of lives
lived in harmony with Creation.

May we, Your servants, increasingly serve.

May we, Your servants, increasingly come to love Your
Creation
as we also increasingly come to love You,

through Christ Jesus,
our Lord.

Amen.

2. The Earth Is the Lord's

The world and all that is in it belong to the Lord;
the earth and all who live on it are his.
—Psalm 24:1 (TEV)

This is one of many Scripture passages emphasizing that the earth is God's. God created the earth and all in it for his own honor and glory. Out of love for humankind, God created us in his image. Our commission: to tend the creation, to be caretakers, trustees, stewards, managers, and even cocreators with God.

There is a significant relationship between our being created in God's image and our responsibility to have "dominion over" the creation (Genesis 1:26, KJV) or to steward it. Listen to God's words as recorded in Genesis 1:26-31 (TEV):

> And now we will make human beings; they will be like us and resemble us. They will have power over the fish, the birds, and all animals, domestic and wild, large and small. So God created human beings, making them to be like himself. He created them male and female, blessed them, and said, "Have many children, so that your descendants will live all over the earth and bring it under their control. I am putting you in charge of the fish, the birds, and all the wild animals. I have provided all kinds of grain and all kinds of fruit for you to eat. . . . God looked at everything he had made, and he was very pleased.

From this account we learn that the creation is good! We are to be caretakers of that good creation. In so doing we bring honor and glory to our Creator—who blesses us.

True worship goes beyond words to deeds. Art wrote the following verses a few years ago to celebrate the creation story and highlight the responsibility given us to care for that creation.

Creator God, We Praise Your Name
Creator God, we praise your name, who framed the world
        on high.
From everlasting you are God; you set in place the sky,
Arranged the stars in swirling space—the sun, the moon
        in proper place,
Then looked upon it all as good, blessed wonder
        of your grace.
Creator God, we praise your name, who formed the morning
        light,
Then separated it from dark and called it day and night.
You gave us work and daily rest, and with your goodness
        to be blessed
To daily now your wonders see and in your presence be.

Creator God, we praise your name, for creatures large
        and small.

You gave them wisdom to succeed, and all else
> that they need,
Then blessed them with your spoken word, in voice of love
> forever heard:
"Be fruitful, multiply, and fill the earth with every kind."

Creator God, we praise your name, who in your likeness
> formed
All people that on earth do dwell—they do your glory tell.
You charged us for the earth to care—for land, the sea,
> and open air,
To love and honor all your works in peace with tender care.

These stanzas emphasize the straightforward command of God: "This is my own good creation, and you are in charge. Love it, care for it, be a cocreator with me!" But in today's world there is evidence that many people have forgotten these words. They don't remember that "the earth is the Lord's" (Psalm 24:1, KJV).

Things have not turned out as God intended. The earth and all its creatures do not live in harmony with the Creator. People have often chosen to violate God's will and live selfishly. They have desired to become gods themselves, to do things their own way. They have become separated from God. This is the Old Testament story!

But God has been gracious. He provided a plan to redeem us from disobedience and sin: he sent his Son. God allowed a fresh beginning, a new start, that we might again be the kind of stewards of the earth that he had originally planned.

Despite the possibility of this new beginning through the life, death, and resurrection of Christ, many of us choose what is right in our own eyes. That is often at the expense of God's good creation. We seem to be driven by what's known as "economic progress." We equate happiness with material wealth. In the process, God's good creation is exploited and degraded. We have not been good managers of the earth.

Many of the hunger, poverty, and justice problems in today's world stem from a neglected or inadequate theology of creation and of the land. We need to rediscover and fully accept the biblical teachings about the land and our relationship to it. These teachings come to us through the Hebrew Scriptures, the Prophets, and the Gospels. Our relationship to the land, to creation, is a moral and ethical matter.

Two primary themes dominate biblical teaching about the land:
- Land is a gift from God.
- That gift is to be received and cared for as a trust.

Earthkeeping Failures

It is quite clear that humans have not heeded the biblical mandate to be good stewards of the earth and its resources. Evidence is not hard to find:
- 1.3 billion of the earth's five billion-plus people are malnourished.
- At least 450 million are chronically hungry.
- Since the beginning of agriculture, half of the earth's food-producing soil has disappeared. By the year 2000, less than 5 percent of the earth's surface will be arable.
- Each year, forests covering half the size of California are destroyed.
- About 800 million people in our world live in absolute poverty.

Why such statistics? These are numbers that illustrate human suffering and the groaning of the earth. They show a global system out of balance because of human decisions. As Gandhi said: "There are sufficient resources on earth to satisfy everyone's need, but not everyone's greed."

The tragic fact is that this hunger, poverty, and exploitation of the earth's resources is unnecessary. The earth is the Lord's. The creation is good. It is able to support the marvelous assortment of living things, including all people, in a society that is just, sustainable, and participatory. A return to the message of the prophets, Christ, and the apostles can produce the kind of world God envisioned when he created it. But we need to make some changes for this to happen.

Earthkeepers' Response

What then are we to do?

• We need to study, pray, and listen to the Holy Spirit to see what the Bible really says about our relationship to God's creation and to each other.

• We need to recognize that appropriate stewardship of the creation is exemplified ultimately in the double love command that is described in Deuteronomy and Leviticus and by Jesus in the Gospels: "Love the Lord your God with all your heart, with all your soul, with all your mind, and with all your strength. . . . Love your neighbor as you love yourself" (Mark 12:30-31, TEV).

• We need to examine our lifestyles to see if our living is compatible with the constraints of nature. A test for each of us might be this: If everyone in God's creation lived as I do, would there be enough to go around? Could the earth survive? Could the needy survive?

• We need to maintain a global perspective of the creation as we live locally in our part of the world. Remember Micah 6:8 (TEV): "The Lord has told us what is good. What he requires of us is this: to do what is just, to show constant love, and to live in humble fellowship with our God."

May God help each of us to be responsible stewards of the creation. For indeed "the earth is the Lord's."

3. New Testament Environmental Ethic

Old Testament teaching on the care of the created world is abundant and clear. God's created order is good. The earth is the Lord's. God's people are to respect it and care for it. The prophets continually warn that human beings cannot selfishly achieve physical affluence without exploiting the created world or oppressing poor people.

Christians, however, derive their ethics mostly from the New Testament. What does the New Testament say about an environmental ethic, about care of the earth, about creation stewardship?

In light of the gross environmental deterioration occurring worldwide today, it is evident that adequate earth stewardship is not being practiced. There is soil erosion, water and air pollution, deforestation, and desertification. Is this because New Testament Christianity lacks an environmental ethic? Surely not, for the theology for such an ethic is indeed present. It is critically important that Christians rediscover that theology if God's created world is to be preserved.

Creation Theology

One theologian who does an excellent job of interpreting a creation theology based on New Testament teaching is Paulos Mar Gregorios. He is a world-respected biblical student from the Indian Orthodox tradition. Gregorios describes this theology in in a recent book edited by Wesley Granberg-Michaelson called *Tending the Garden*. His chapter is called "New Testament Foundations for Understanding the Creation" (pages 83-92).

Gregorios identifies basic ecological principles in three important New Testament passages. The first passage, from Romans 8:18-25, he translates:

> For the created order awaits with eager longing, with neck outstretched, the full manifestation of the children of God. . . . The creator made the creation contingent, in his ordering, upon hope; for the creation itself has something to look forward to—namely, to be freed from its present enslavement to disintegration. The creation itself is to share in the freedom, in the glorious and undying goodness, of the children of God. For we know how the whole creation up till now has been groaning together in agony, in a common pain. And not just the non-human created order—even we ourselves, as Christians who have received the advance gift of the Holy Spirit, are now groaning within ourselves, for we are also waiting—waiting for the transformation of our bodies for the full experience of our adoption as God's children.

The basic ecological principle Gregorios derived from these words is simply stated: "Human redemption can be understood only as an integral part of the redemption of the whole creation."

Redemption of Creation

For too long, Christians have been conditioned to understand redemption in Christ primarily in terms of personal salvation. But Gregorios claims that the writings of both Paul and John "strongly affirm the redemption of the whole creation—cosmic redemption—or the participation of all creation in the liberation of humanity from the bondage of sin and death. The whole creation— not just a few souls—has been redeemed and reconciled in Christ."

To develop a genuine Christian environmental ethic, a new understanding of the redemption in Christ Jesus will have to take into account "personal and corporate salvation; spiritual reality and material reality in the creation and the incarnation; the created order as the object and field of the redeeming order; and the human person as integrally related to the whole cosmos."

Gregorios translates Colossians 1:15-23:

> He, Christ, the Beloved Son, is the manifest presence of the unmanifest God. He is the Elder Brother of all things created, for it was by him and in him that all things were created. . . . All things were created through him, by him, in him. But he himself is before all things; in him they consist and subsist; he is the head of the body, the Church. He is the New Beginning, the Firstborn from the dead; thus he becomes in all respects preeminent. For it was God's good pleasure that in Christ all fullness should dwell; it is through him and in him that all things are to be reconciled and reharmonized. . . . So all things in the visible earth and in the invisible heaven should dwell together in him. . . . You have heard the good news, the good news declared not only to men and women on earth, but to all created beings under heaven.

Gregorios observes: "Christ himself should be seen in his three principal relationships: (1) to members incorporated into his body; (2) to the human race; and (3) to the other than human orders of created existence in a many-planed universe. Each of these is related to the other."

Christ Fulfilling Creation

Christians often think of Christ as being separate from the world, from culture. But, according to Paul in this Scripture, Christ is not an abstract or purely spiritual entity. He is incarnate. He took on an earthly body, becoming part of the created order while remaining unchanged as one of the Trinity—the Creator. He is one of us. All parts of the creation are now reconciled to Christ. The created order is to be set free and to share in the "glorious freedom of the children of God." Gregorios believes that Christian theology's weakness "has been its failure to recognize the wider scope of the redemption beyond the individual soul or person. We must move beyond personal salvation to declare and teach the three basic dimensions of redemption."

Gregorios translates John 1:1-5:

> At the source-spring of all, the Logos [Word] is and was. The Logos is God's . . . and the Logos is God. It is this Logos that in the beginning was face to face with God. It is through the Logos that all existing things have come to exist. Without him not a single thing could have come into being. In him was also life. Life is light in human beings. The light shines in the midst of darkness, and the darkness has not comprehended or overcome the light.

The Orthodox scholar's third ecological principle is this: "Christ and the Holy Spirit are related to the whole created order in three ways—by creating it, by redeeming it, and finally by fulfilling it in the last great consummation."

It is noted here that the act of creation is a corporate act of the Trinity. Nothing came into being without Christ and the Holy Spirit. The creative energy of God is the true being of all that exists; matter is that spirit or energy in physical form. Therefore, we should regard our environment as the energy of God in a form that is accessible to our senses.

Earthkeepers' Response

In summary, the created order, the universe, is to be respected (not worshiped) as the order that has given birth to us, sustains us, and will be the framework for our existence when the whole process of creation-redemption has been completed. We are to respect the created order both because it comes from God and is sustained by him and because it is the place of our origin, growth, and fulfillment as human beings. We therefore have a responsibility to tend the creation as we use it for our own development. However, we must also respect it in its own right as a tangible manifestation of God's creative energy. We must cooperate with God in bringing out the full magnificence of the created world as reflecting the glory of the Creator.

Only as we combine these New Testament understandings of the created order with those of the wisdom literature of the Old Testament can modern Christians develop an appropriate creation theology—one that produces an appropriate environmental ethic for living in today's world. Until we begin to live out this new ethic, Christians will continue to be implicated with all other people in hastening the environmental degradation rampant on God's earth today.

4. Ecojustice: A Theology of Ecology

God looked at everything he had made,
and he was very pleased.
　　　　—Genesis 1:31 (TEV)

Ecojustice is a relatively new term for Christians. It combines the concept of *ecological living* with that of *economic justice* for the earth and all its people.

Ecology is the science that deals with living organisms, their interactions with each other and with the environment. Ecologists study organisms, populations, communities, ecosystems, and the entire earth's biosphere. One concern of ecology is the appropriate place of humankind in this web of life.

Limited Energy

Like all natural sciences, ecology depends upon earth's basic laws of matter and energy. Materially, everything must go somewhere. In any normal physical or chemical process, matter is neither created nor destroyed but merely changed from one form to another. Likewise, for energy, the first law of thermodynamics is that in any ordinary physical or chemical process, energy is neither created nor destroyed. It is only changed from one form to another.

The second law of thermodynamics concerning energy, however, points to useful work. Some of the energy is always degraded to a more dispersed and less useful form. Although the quantity of energy stays the same, the quality is degraded and essentially lost for use by living things. *Entropy* is a term used to refer to this phenomenon. This loss of useful energy in life activities is an important concept, one that is often overlooked in our system of growth economics. It means that energy available for human activities is indeed limited.

All new energy for life comes to earth by way of the sun. Only small amounts of this energy can be captured by green plants and stored in food and fiber. Some was stored in fossil fuels many years ago, providing coal, petroleum, and natural gas. Modern industrial society is based primarily on the readily available, easily accessible stored energy of fossil fuels. Science and industry sometimes give the erroneous impression that nature can be manipulated, bypassed, or circumvented, that something can be made from nothing with little effort. This is just not so. There is no free lunch in nature. If any work is done, action taken, or product manufactured, energy is expended. Some part of nature, or someone, has to pay.

Ecological Crisis

Because of overpopulation and overconsumption by people today, an ecological crisis has developed. The Lord's earth is becoming environmentally degraded. Such processes as deforestation, desertification, air and water pollution, soil erosion, and toxic waste buildup are parts of this degradation.

Ecologists agree that any industrialized society expecting to survive on a finite earth must be based on recycling matter and reducing the use of energy. The alternative, a society of ever-expanding growth, runs counter to the second law of thermodynamics. John Carmody, in his book *Ecology and Religion*, puts it this way: "The ecological crisis comes down to simple blindness; we do not see how the world really works. Especially in the industrially advanced nations, we are living in blatant contradiction to the way the world really works, ignoring the basic laws of matter and energy" (p. 12).

Many people do not want to see how the world really works. They do not accept the laws of nature. They allow greed and envy and wishful thinking to blind them to nature's reality.

William Gibson, in a chapter on ecojustice in the book *For Creation's Sake*, comments on the ecological crisis:

> Concern about ecology in our time arises out of the realization that nature places limitations upon human behavior. The limits were always there written into the natural order as God created it. But the recognition of those limits is a distinctly contemporary occurrence, coming after several centuries of distinctly modern disregard for limits. The limits have become apparent as never before in history precisely because they were disregarded until the global consequences of disregard became unmistakable (p. 17).

Ecojustice

Ecojustice is concerned with reversing the ecological crisis and at the same time securing justice for the poor. It's about responsible *earth* stewardship as well as responsible *person* stewardship. Ecojustice is what Jesus was talking about when he recommended and practiced a simple lifestyle. But it is a concept that the modern

Christian church has largely ignored as it conformed to the materialistic society surrounding it.

During the 1973 and 1979 oil crises, there was a general reawakening to ecojustice principles. This led to considerable environmental awareness in the industrialized world. Christians, too, began to recognize the importance of renewable energy—solar, wood, biomass, wind, water power—and the problems with nonrenewable energy—oil, coal, nuclear, natural gas.

In the 1980s, interest in environmental awareness, steady state economics, and more-with-less living appeared to be diminishing among the public. A major reason was the free enterprise growth economics promoted by U.S. and Canadian government leaders in that decade. People were told that there were no limits, that they did not need to pay attention to natural laws. They were told bigger is better; growth is necessary; work hard, and you can lift yourself up by your own bootstraps.

Simple answers have been given to complex issues. Apparently, that is what most people like. They are led to believe again that they can have their cake and eat it, too. The message is that they can have growth economics and an overconsumptive society and still have a healthy earth. But that is not possible. The ecological crisis has not abated since 1973. The state of the world's people has not improved appreciably since 1973. They have been led on in blind disregard of the reality of the continuing crisis.

A 1984 binational consultation in Toronto (Ontario, Canada) focused on acid rain. Scientists and theologians from 25 Canadian and U.S. church bodies developed a contemporary framework for theological reflection and for teaching ecojustice.

Theirs was a significant statement—one that should help Christians rediscover a theology of ecology that is relevant to environmental issues in today's world.

Our Theological Understanding

1. God as Creator of heaven and earth and all earth's creatures looks lovingly upon all the works of creation and pronounces them very good. God continues to care for creation and to fill all the creatures with good things.

2. God as Deliverer acts to protect, restore, and redeem the earth and its creatures. These have become co-victims with all humanity, victims of the sinful pride and greed that seek unwarranted mastery over the natural and social orders, and the sinful sloth and carelessness that refuse responsibility for understanding and serving God's world.

3. God as Jesus Christ has acted to reunite all things and to call the human creation back to the role of the steward, the responsible servant, who as God's representative cares for creation and acts in society for the sustenance and fulfillment of the one human family.

4. The Creator-Deliverer acts in the ecological-social crisis of our time to demonstrate that same divine love which was manifested in the cross of Christ; and we as a covenant people are called to increase our stewardship, in relation both to nature and to political economy, to a level commensurate with the peril and the promise with which God confronts us in this crisis.

5. Human stewardship is not a dominion of mastery. It is a dominion of unequivocal love for this world. It is to be exercised with respect for the integrity of natural systems and for the limits that nature places on economic growth and material consumption.

Earthkeepers' Response

The statement concludes with these suggestions for action:

As stewards:

• We seek a political economy directed to the protection of the poor and to the sufficient and sustainable sustenance of all people.

• We accept the responsibility of using political processes to check the abuses of power that would otherwise continue to victimize the earth and the poor.

• We insist that the costs of restoring the polluted environment and of structuring sustainable practices and institutions be distributed equitably throughout our society.

(from the Toronto Consultation on Acid Rain, January 1984)

We hope more and more Christians will include the concept of ecojustice as a fundamental tenet of their faith and practice. Could Paul have meant ecojustice in Ephesians 1:10 (TEV) when he describes a "plan, which God will complete when the time is right, . . . to bring all creation together, everything in heaven and on earth, with Christ as head"?

5. Ten Global Issues for Christian Reflection

As our world of five billion people becomes increasingly interdependent, more global issues emerge that are complex and interrelated. Our perspective is that of Christians trained in science, who did international research in the areas of hunger, poverty, and injustice. We have identified ten key issues facing humankind as the twentieth century comes to a close.

We rank and briefly describe these situations, starting with ones that seem to have the most global significance:

1. *Environmental degradation*

We consider the insidious destruction of the natural systems that support all life on earth to be the number one global problem. Overpopulation in developing countries and overconsumption and waste of natural resources in industrialized countries is putting great stress on the earth's ecosystems—land, air, and water. We have forgotten that the earth is the Lord's and our mandate is to maintain it for his glory. Who else on earth can manage the creation?

2. *The worldwide arms race and the nuclear threat*

In 1988 an estimated $1 trillion was spent on arms. (That amount is equal to a stack of $1,000 bills 67 miles high.) This money is sorely needed for human development programs and to reverse environmental damage. The two superpowers spend over half the world's arms budget and are responsible for two-thirds of the arms exports to the Third World.

Some people might call the threat of nuclear annihilation the world's number one problem. That's understandable, but the nuclear problem is so apparent and so focused today that we believe it will be resolved. Degradation of the environment is so subtle that we believe it constitutes more danger than the nuclear threat. Of course, the arms buildup contributes to environmental destruction, too. War and military preparation for war are the world's worst destroyers of natural resources.

3. *Blind adherence to political-economic systems that are incompatible with natural laws*

Most present economic systems—capitalist, communist, or socialist—disregard fundamental laws of nature. They pay little attention to ecological principles, such as "everything is connected to everything else," "everything must go somewhere," "nature knows best," and "there is no such thing as a free lunch."

Because of this disregard, our societies are building up dangerous environmental debts. Present political-economic systems promote an untenable free-lunch mentality. When implemented, these systems exploit nature or people or both.

4. *The hunger scandal*

Estimates of the hungry in our world today range from 450 million to more than one billion persons. At the same time industrialized countries are awash in grain. The major problem is that industrialized countries produce food at a cost beyond what hungry people can afford to pay. There are many other issues related to hunger, including food and agriculture policy, poverty, loss of crop land, access to land, policies of multinationals, and export cropping.

5. *Providing full and meaningful employment for all who are able to work*

This must be done without further destruction to the natural resource base—an incredible challenge. The World Resources Institute describes this problem as its basic purpose: "How can we meet basic human needs and nurture economic growth without undermining the natural resources on which life, economic vitality, and international security depend?"

Other related issues include world trade structure and monetary systems, automation and jobs, and the military-industrial complex and jobs.

6. *The rapidly increasing gap between the rich and the poor*

The economic gulf between the haves and the have-nots, both among and within countries, is increasing. Access to improved communication through computers and other technology by the wealthy and powerful allows them to exert control over the poor. Failure to narrow this gap will result in further injustice to the poor.

7. *Inappropriate food and agricultural policies worldwide*

Industrial agriculture as practiced in the developed world and introduced into the Third World during the green revolution is not sustainable in the long term. It uses up limited supplies of fossil fuels, it degrades the soil, and it pollutes the environment. The extension of industrial agriculture by use of modern biotechnology and genetic engineering (a new green revolution?) will not solve the food problem in the long term. A food and agriculture policy is needed that promotes production within the constraints of nature's rules—a sustainable agriculture.

8. *The family-farm crisis*

In the U.S. this involves farm bankruptcy, concentration of farmland ownership, loss of farmland by blacks, and deterioration of rural communities. Worldwide, industrialization of agriculture and cash cropping for export forces peasant farmers off the land. This results in migration to Third-World cities where these farmers are more economically and socially vulnerable.

9. *The human population explosion*

This is related to all the other issues. The expected doubling of the world's population in 40 years will put increasing stress on political-economic systems worldwide. The earth cannot sustain the present rate of human population growth—or growth in consumption—indefinitely. Overpopulation, overconsumption, and poverty continue to be important issues in need of resolution as the twenty-first century approaches.

10. *The colonial legacy, multinational corporations, and Third-World political leaders*

In Asia, Africa, and Latin America, European colonists have

consolidated their earlier power by doing development via multi-national corporations in conjunction with the new elite in those countries. More often than not, the elite are part of an oppressive military regime which controls the poor like the colonials used to.

Other issues that have global dimensions include human rights, racism, sexism, problems of the elderly and the disabled, the hazardous waste problem, abortion, health care of the poor, and criminal justice.

Earthkeepers' Response

Christians want to follow the example of Jesus—to help those who are in need. How do we best help the needy? By getting to know them first, of course, but also by knowing the reasons behind their need. As we understand how many issues are connected, we see more clearly how many of our decisions affect the poor who may be across town or across the seas.

6. I, Too, Have a Dream

God created human beings and assigned them
to manage the earth, plants, animals, and birds.
And God saw that everything he had made was very good.
       —based on Genesis 1:26-31

I, Jocele, have a dream that one day we, too, will see all that God has created as good. We will live in such ways that word and deed are one. We will work toward that day as we farm in more sustainable ways, plant trees that purify the air, cultivate our urban gardens, and make a habit of walking short distances so fewer parking lots represent the last harvest on the land.

I have a dream that humankind will more fully understand what it means to live in covenant with God. Because the Israelites broke God's covenant law, the land mourned (Hosea 4). But listen to the promise of the Lord for the time following Israel's punishment and restoration, as related by Hosea:

> In that day I will make a covenant for them
>> with the beasts of the field and birds of the air
>> and the creatures that move along the ground.
> Bow and sword and battle
>> I will abolish from the land,
>> so that all may lie down in safety.
> I will betroth you to me forever;
>> I will betroth you in righteousness and justice,
>> in love and compassion.
> I will betroth you in faithfulness,
>> and you will acknowledge the Lord. (Hosea 2:18-20)

I have a dream that we will be faithful caretakers of the land, the vegetation, the animals, and the people when we see ourselves as a part of the covenant between the Creator and the created. We will assume our roles as cocreators with God as we give space for the creation to grow, to multiply, to be regenerated, and to develop in the ways that were intended when God placed natural limits in the total plan of creation.

I dream that we will respect the dignity of all humankind as we live in covenant. Decisions will be made, so no one is harmed. Those persons with access to technology will limit those skills, so those who have less access to technology will not be overpowered and left far behind. Those lacking technological benefits will receive their fair share, so their lives will be enriched with greater access to food, shelter, and a sense of self-worth.

Listen again to the word of the Lord. On Mount Sinai the Lord gave Moses this message for the Israelites:

> When you enter the land I am going to give you, the land itself must observe a sabbath to the Lord. For six years sow your fields, and for six years prune your vineyards and gather their crops. But in the seventh year the land is to have a sabbath of rest, a sabbath to the Lord. . . . Consecrate the fiftieth year and proclaim liberty throughout the land to all its inhabitants. It shall be a jubilee for you; each one of you is to return to his family property and each to his

own clan. The fiftieth year shall be a jubilee for you; do not sow and do not reap what grows of itself or harvest the untended vines. For it is a jubilee and is to be holy for you; eat only what is taken from the fields. . . . The land must not be sold permanently, because the land is mine and you are but aliens and my tenants. (Leviticus 25:2-4a, 10-12, 23)

I have a dream that one day we will be wise enough to understand this passage. We will care for the land and resources in such a way that all will have access to it and its fruits.

In that day we will stand arm in arm with those who have lost their land, grieving for what once was. As they consider the "if onlys" that might have kept them from this situation, we will love them and walk with them. We will help them as God gives us wisdom.

In turn, we will accept the outstretched hands of brothers and sisters. They mean to comfort and give encouragement when we are depressed and in need.

We will stand beside those who are caught in the midst of the struggle. Some must find new jobs because farming is no longer viable. They may be children who will not be able to follow footsteps of fathers and mothers who have farmed the land. We will help them retrain and find fulfillment as they continue to serve God and other human beings, whether on the land or in the factory.

We will take time to listen. In turn, there will be someone listening to us.

We will stand beside those who have not been touched firsthand by a changing economy or changing farm practices. They struggle to understand the hurts of others, as they continue without being touched by financial and emotional distress. They seek to understand that all persons are interdependent and have a special relationship to the environment, as they begin to reach out to the problems of the rest of the world.

I dream that we will share our resources, our time and compassion, empathizing as we serve and worship the same God who created us all.

I dream that godly moral standards so long connected with people of the land will be espoused by God's people no matter where they live—in the city high-rise building, the suburban sprawl, the picturesque village, or the productive farmstead. James speaks of one enviable characteristic of the farmer; "See how the farmer waits for the land to yield its valuable crop and how *patient* he is for the fall and spring rains. You too, be *patient* and *stand firm*" (James 5:7b-8a, emphasis added).

I pray that we will truly be able to live in such a way that we look to God for our daily bread, not depending solely on the strength of our hands, nor the skills of our minds. We will trust God to provide the manna of daily living, as he supplied the children of Israel with manna in the wilderness. They received each day just as much as they could eat. I dream that we will savor our daily bread.

I dream that the 1.3 billion hungry people in world will no longer be hungry. I dream that there will be changed people and changed systems, so the ability we do have to feed everyone on earth can be used. I dream that because we will share of our plenty to meet their immediate needs, the world's 512 million starving people will no longer be on the verge of dying.

Is it too much to dream that this vision can be implemented beginning today? Isaiah spoke eloquently to this when he said, "Stop doing wrong, learn to do right! Seek justice, encourage the oppressed. Defend the cause of the fatherless, plead the cause of the widow" (Isaiah 1:16-17).

When, Lord, will we cease to only dream?

I dream that Ethiopian farmers, for example, will again live in a land without conflict and increasing impoverishment. Then they can take charge of their years of plenty and years of famine, balancing out their food supply as they learned to do in the past.

I dream that the Christian church, with its many dedicated members, will take up the challenge and become an instrument of change. In that role, the church as God's people will courageously be a prophetic voice in a world that has lost its course.

I dream and I pray that we will be able to live more fully in harmony with God, with all creation, and with our fellow human beings. Not as master and slave, landowner and tenant, farmer and factory worker, but as brothers and sisters.

Lord, forgive our willingness to ignore your truths
    and the realities of today's world,
our arrogant spirits in relationships with your children,
and our greediness as we use more than our fair share
    of the abundance of the land, the air,
    and the waters upon the earth.

May we choose a way of life that is in harmony
    with the environment around us.
May we live our daily lives in such a way
    that our decisions and our activities
    express the praise our lips so easily speak to you,
our Creator, Sustainer, and Savior.

May we live in the hope of the light
    that surrounds the birth of your Son.
May we be a part of the rightness and justice
    that will be accomplished by the zeal of the Almighty,
as we step aside to remember
    the earth is the Lord's,
    and we are God's people. Amen.

Discussion Questions

1. To what extent are Christians responsible for present environmental degradation on earth? Defend your answer.

2. Verbalize a simple, basic theology of creation that is supported by Scripture and provides an appropriate base for ecological living.

3. Genesis 1:26 refers to humankind as "having dominion over" or intended to "rule over" the natural world. What does this mean? How do you interpret that verse?

4. Examine carefully the three ecological principles Gregorios draws from Scripture. To what extent do you agree/disagree with his interpretation?

5. If possible, study chapter 7 of Milo Kauffman's book *Stewards of God* (listed below). Compare Kauffman's scriptural interpretation with that of Gregorios.

6. In the chapter on ecojustice, the "no free lunch in nature" principle is described. To what extent do you accept the

interpretation there? If you accept the principle, how will you relate it to your lifestyle?

7. What is ecojustice? To what extent do you think it is possible for all people to simultaneously have worthwhile employment, not degrade the environment, and live a quality life?

8. Of the ten global issues discussed, which do you think are most important? Least important? Are your top ten issues listed there?

9. What is your dream for a society such as God intended? Verbalize it.

Resources

Austin, Richard Cartwright. Environmental theology set, making a comprehensive, systematic Christian statement. Published at Louisville by Westminster/John Knox Press: *Baptized into the Wilderness: A Christian Perspective on John Muir*, 1987. *Beauty of the Land: Awakening the Senses*, 1988. *Hope for the Land: Nature in the Bible*, 1988. *Reclaiming America: Restoring Nature to Culture*, 1990.

Carmody, John. *Ecology and Religion: Toward a New Christian Theology of Nature*. Ramsey, N.J.: Paulist Press, 1973. Chapter 1.

Cesaretti, C. A., and Stephen Commins, eds. *Let the Earth Bless the Lord*. New York: Harper Row, 1981. Meditations and essays on earth stewardship.

Evans, Bernard F., and Gregory Cusack. *Theology of the Land*. Collegeville, Minn.: The Liturgical Press, 1987. Five theologians present essays on land stewardship.

Granberg-Michaelson, Wesley. *Ecology and Life: Accepting Our Environmental Responsibility*. Waco, Tex.: Word, Inc., 1988. Good biblical interpretation of environmental issues.

Granberg-Michaelson, Wesley, ed. *Tending the Garden: Essays on the Gospel of the Earth*. Grand Rapids, Mich.: Eerdmans, 1987. Nine essays that relate to creation theology.

Granberg-Michaelson, Wesley. *A Worldly Spirituality: The Call to Take Care of the Earth*. San Francisco: Harper and Row, 1984. An evangelical interpretation of creation theology, on creation destroyed, creation redeemed, and creation restored.

Hallman, David G. *Caring for Creation*. Winfield, B.C.: Woodlake Books, Inc., 1990. A primer for environmental concerns. Considers the pervasive theology that has contributed to the abuse of the earth, from a Canadian perspective.

Hessel, Dieter T., ed. *For Creation's Sake: Preaching, Ecology, and Justice*. Philadelphia: Geneva Press, 1982. Essays by prominent theologians relating biblical justice and ecology.

Kauffman, Milo. *Stewards of God*. Scottdale, Pa.: Herald Press, 1975. An Anabaptist interpretation of creation theology in chapter 7.

North American Conference on Christianity and Ecology Document. In three parts, with a prayer of thanksgiving and confession, a theology of creation and redemption, and ethics of faith and action. Available free from MCC U.S. Global Education Office, Box 500, Akron, PA 17501-0500.

PART TWO

Environmental Degradation

Hazardous Waste

The discharge of toxic substances or other substances that exceed the capacity of the environment to render them harmless must be halted in order to ensure that serious or irreversible damage is not inflicted upon ecosystems. The just struggles of the peoples of all countries against pollution should be supported.
> —United Nations Conference on
> Human Environment, 1984

The air is precious to the red man for all things share the same breath—the beast, the tree, the man, they all share the same breath. The white man does not seem to notice the air he breathes. Like a man dying for many days, he is numb to the stench. But if we sell you our land, you must remember that the air is precious to us, that the air shares its spirit with all the life it supports. The wind that gave our grandfather his first breath also receives his last sigh. And the wind must also give our children the spirit of life. And if we sell you our land, you must keep it apart and sacred, as a place where even the white man can go to taste the wind that is sweetened by the meadow's flowers.

You must teach your children that the ground beneath their feet is the ashes of our grandfathers. So that they will respect the land, tell your children that the earth is rich with the lives of our kin. Teach your children what we have taught our children, that the earth is our mother. Whatever befalls the earth befalls the sons of the earth. If men spit upon the ground, they spit upon themselves.
> —Chief Seattle of the Duwamish and Suquamish, 1855

7. Toxic Waste: "This Earth Is Precious to God"

This earth is precious to God and to harm the earth is to heap contempt on its Creator. . . . Continue to contaminate your bed and you will one night suffocate in your own waste.
—Chief Seattle, in a speech before signing
a treaty with white people in 1855

The respected Indian orator quoted above was well aware of one simple law of ecology: everything must go somewhere. He sensed that the industrialization Europeans brought to North America was not fully compatible with the natural world he so deeply understood and loved. Chief Seattle's fears are being widely realized today as we see environmental destruction increasing around us.

Poisoned by Waste

We live in one of the most productive industrial societies in history. Our lives are comfortable, but the wastes produced from our economic system are enormous. We have heedlessly dumped industrial chemicals, agricultural poisons, and radioactive wastes into our lakes, streams, and groundwater. We have contaminated our nests and are now suffocating in our own waste.

We still live largely with the frontier mentality that says we can simply throw unwanted materials away. But there is no *away* anymore. Conventional wisdom has said the "solution to pollution is dilution," but dilution has reached the limit in many instances. We have scattered wastes in hundreds of thousands of landfills across the country, 50,000 of which contain toxic materials. Up to 37,000 of them may be contaminating groundwater, according to the National Association of Counties. In addition, an estimated 181,000 pits and ponds are used to store wastes. Of the 26,000 that contain toxic industrial chemicals, 87 percent lie directly atop vulnerable underground water supplies.

According to Jonathan King in his recent book *Troubled Water*, "each year the U.S. injects some 10 billion gallons of sewage, radioactive waste, chemicals, and brine deep into the earth. Now these poisons are coming back to haunt us, in our groundwater and the thousands of wells" it serves. In his introduction, King reports further startling facts about our drinking water:

• In its 1982 survey of large public water systems served by groundwater, the U.S. Environmental Protection Agency (EPA) found 45 percent of them contaminated with organic chemicals.

• According to the EPA's survey of U.S. rural households, two-thirds used drinking water that violated at least one of its health standards.

• In California, pesticides have tainted the drinking water of nearly one million people.

• In New Jersey, every major aquifer (groundwater formation) is affected by chemical contaminants.

Many analysts think that chemical contamination of our water supplies has become the most serious environmental problem of our time. U.S. Representative Mike Synar of Oklahoma warns that "the next great domestic crisis we may face as a nation is a water crisis and . . . its solution may be more expensive and more elusive than the energy crisis" (*Troubled Water*, p. xi).

Polluted Groundwater

Pollution affecting groundwater is the most troubling problem. Ninety-six percent of our water is in aquifers underground. Because this water is not visible, it is given little thought. Yet ground-water provides drinking water for half the U.S. population and more than 90 percent of rural residents.

Groundwater was once thought to be a pure source of water, naturally filtered and cleansed by soil percolations. But recently it has been found that once chemicals percolate down through the soil and get into the underground water supply, they do not readily disperse, settle out, or degrade. Robert Harris, a hazardous waste expert from Princeton University says, "For all practical purposes, groundwater contamination is irreversible by natural forces."

Many industrial and agricultural chemicals have been found in groundwater—chemicals from hazardous waste sites, heavy metals, radioactive substances from mining, gasoline from underground storage tanks, pesticides and nitrates from agriculture, salt from road deicing, brine from oil and gas well drilling, and nitrates and bacteria from leaky septic tanks.

The extent of groundwater contamination in the U.S. is not known. The EPA requires public water systems to check for only a few of the industrial chemicals commonly found in groundwater. No testing at all is required for the millions of private wells.

Even though there has been increased environmental awareness since the formation of the EPA in 1970, groundwater contamination has continued to escalate. In the 1970s, the EPA and environmentalists focused attention on controlling the discharge of pollution in surface waters, such as the push to clean up Lake Erie and Ohio's Cuyahoga River. Meanwhile, billions of tons of chemical wastes in landfills, dumps, pits, and ponds were slowly seeping through the ground into the water table.

EPA officials have claimed ignorance of this problem. Former EPA administrator William Ruckelshause said in 1984, "Ten years ago, for all practical purposes, we were unaware that there was a hazardous waste problem! Burial, after all, was the symbol of ultimate disposal. Groundwater was the very symbol of purity" (*Troubled Water*, p. xiii).

It took Love Canal and Times Beach to publicize the threat from land disposal of hazardous waste. Even so, EPA, the U.S. Congress, and the public have moved slowly. Often "clean-up" is done by moving waste from one site to another or one medium to another. There is now a high price to pay for the years of neglect and mismanagement of toxic waste disposal and water supplies. Joe Hirschhorn, a hazardous waste management expert at the Congressional Office of Technology Assessment (OTA), calls it "the environmental debt." We will end up paying that debt either with money or our health or both.

Earthkeepers' Response

There are alternatives to hazardous waste landfills. Much waste can be recycled or chemically or physically treated to render it harmless. There are proven ways to reduce the amount of waste generated. Incineration of garbage and other wastes is becoming popular in the U.S. Although it does reduce volume, it is not without problems. Associated with the process are toxic emissions and other air pollutants. Incineration may also discourage the use of more ecologically sound recycling programs. Responsible lifestyles using renewable resources and recycling can help reverse past trends.

One thing is certain. In the future we will have to more fully respect God's patterns of creation to which Chief Seattle referred when he "sold" that land to us in 1854. Nature is impartial. We reap what we sow. Everything must go somewhere. To live requires energy. The more energy we use, the more wastes we produce. There is no free lunch in nature.

As one looks at the message of the Bible and the teachings of Jesus, the above themes are apparent for those with "eyes to see and ears to hear."

It is time for us to look, listen, and stop harming the earth and heaping contempt upon the Creator.

8. Pesticides Threaten Food, Water, and People

Chemical pesticides have been vigorously promoted as indispensable components of modern food production. Food production has indeed increased, but so have important negative side effects. The misuse of pesticides may be pushing nature beyond its capacity to sustain life.

Pesticides include insecticides (insect killers), herbicides (weed killers), miticides (mite killers), fungicides (fungus killers), and others. According to Sandra Postel in Worldwatch Paper 79 (September 1987), pesticide use in U.S. agriculture nearly tripled between 1965 and 1985. Farmers applied 390,000 tons of pesticides in 1985.

Pesticides pose an increasingly ominous health threat to people in three ways: in residues on consumer foods, through groundwater contamination, and in their handling and application.

Pesticides and Cancer

"Pesticides in 15 Common Foods May Cause 20,000 Cancers Yearly" is the title of an article by Mary Painter in *Food Monitor* (Summer 1987). The article analyzes a report released by the U.S. National Academy of Sciences (May 1987) on pesticide residues on foods. The two-year study by a special committee of the academy, the National Research Council, concludes that 15 foods contaminated by pesticides used in their production pose the greatest risk of cancer. The foods, in order of most to least cancer risk, are tomatoes, beef, potatoes, oranges, lettuce, apples, peaches, pork, wheat, soybeans, beans, carrots, chicken, grapes, and corn.

The National Resources Defense Council (NRDC), a respected, nationwide environmental organization, conducted a 1983 study in which ten kinds of fresh produce sold in San Francisco markets were analyzed for pesticide residue. Forty-four percent of the 71 fruit and vegetable samples contained residues of 19 different pesticides. Although many of the pesticides detected were in amounts below EPA tolerance, the NRDC believes EPA standards are debatable. NRDC claims that the EPA allows the presence of cancer-producing pesticides in food, despite the absence of a proven safe level of exposure to carcinogens.

Restraints for Pesticide Use

Although there are government regulations on pesticides, many officials and environmentalists see a great need for revision. Painter refers to a report in *The New York Times* (22 May 1987) that says, "the end of the food chain is also the end of a pesticide chain that starts in the factory where they are produced and moves through the fields where workers can be exposed, into underground drinking water supplies and finally into the wholesale and retail markets before they reach home. There appears to be a broad agreement among government officials as well as environmentalists that the current laws and rules are so cumbersome and inefficient that they leave people, animals, and the environment insufficiently protected along the entire length of the chain."

Pesticides in the U.S. are regulated by the Federal Insecticide, Fungicide, and Rodenticide law adopted in 1947, rewritten in 1972, and reauthorized in 1988. Currently the EPA may impose fairly strict health requirements on new chemicals coming on the market, but the process is lengthy, expensive, and cumbersome. The 1972 revision required EPA to analyze pre-1972 law pesticides, focusing on 600 active ingredients. This has not been done. By 1984, the EPA had reviewed only 76 of them. In 1985, the EPA had studied, researched, and registered less than one percent of present commercial pesticides (Jonathan King in *Troubled Waters*).

The lack of sufficient testing of pesticides is true for other synthetic organic toxic compounds, with 500 to 1,000 new formulations introduced by the chemical industry each year. Synthetic compounds impose more of a risk than natural ones, which the ecosystem can break down. Postel writes that "the National Research Council estimates that no information on the toxic effects is available for 79 percent of the more than 48,500 chemicals listed in EPA's inventory of toxic substances. Fewer than a fifth have been tested for acute effects, and fewer than a tenth for chronic, reproductive or mutagenic effects."

Poisoned Food

Some imported foods have heavy pesticide residues. Many pesticides banned in the U.S. are distributed by a network of multinational chemical corporations to developing countries. In *Circle of Poison,* David Weir and Mark Shapiro list the following among pesticides which are banned in the U.S. but contaminate imported food: DDT, benzene hexachloride, lindane, dieldren, and heptachlor.

The U.S. Food and Drug Administration (FDA) is charged with monitoring imported foods for toxic residues. This enormous task is apparently not well done. A paragraph in the book *Pills, Pesticides and Profits*, edited by Ruth Norris and A. Karim Ahmed, illustrates the problem:

> The FDA estimates that one-tenth of the food imported into the U.S. contains illegal residues of pesticides. That figure may be low. In its 1979 report the General Accounting Office revealed that FDA analytical methods *could not detect* 178 pesticides for which tolerances have been established. Nor can FDA testers assure consumers that imported food is free from some 130 commonly used pesticides for which tolerances have not yet been set. The true extent of pesticide residues returning by way of imported food simply is not known.

Poisoned Groundwater

A second consequence of overuse of pesticides is groundwater contamination. Increasingly, groundwater is becoming infiltrated with pesticide residues. Systematic monitoring of groundwater has not yet been completed, but there is enough evidence of toxic water contamination to warrant concern. Sandra Postel quotes a 1985 U.S. EPA Groundwater Status Report that found the groundwater of at least 23 states was contaminated with 17 different pesticides. Two of the most widely used herbicides—alachlor and atrazine—were the most frequently detected chemicals in this study. Tests have shown alachlor to cause cancer in laboratory animals, making it a possible human carcinogen.

States with the best groundwater monitoring programs in the U.S. (California, New York, and Iowa), have found the greatest number of pesticide contamination incidents in water. No doubt more extensive monitoring in other states would reveal more contamination. Iowa studies show that more than one-quarter of its residents drink water contaminated with pesticides.

In the U.S., researchers Elsabeth Nielsen and Linda Lee examined county level hydrogeologic data along with figures on pesticide use. They concluded that about one-third of all counties in the lower 48 states are vulnerable to groundwater pesticide contamination. Based on this study, nearly 50 million U.S. residents—most of them in rural areas—are potentially at risk of exposure to pesticide-contaminated water.

Poisoned Workers

A third consequence of pesticide use concerns the people who manufacture and use them. According to Worldwatch Paper 79 (September 1987), "between 400,000 and 2 million pesticide poisonings occur worldwide each year, most of them among farmers in developing countries." Those users may not have access to protective clothing and not be able to read the warning labels.

From 10,000 to 40,000 deaths from these poisonings are estimated to occur. One can only estimate the number of cancers, birth defects, and other ailments occurring from pesticide exposure to handlers, farmers, and farm laborers.

Evidence of a direct link between farmers using large quantities of pesticide and cancer occurrence is growing. A recent study, *Farming and Malignant Lymphoma* (a form of cancer), is described in the *Cleveland Plain Dealer* (11 October 1987). The study was done with farmers in Hancock County, Ohio, by the National Institute for Occupational Safety and Health. Herbicide usage in Hancock County has been heavy compared with Ohio as a whole. The researchers found a dramatic increase in fatal cancers among white males who have farmed in Hancock County. The death rate was about 74 percent above the national average between 1960 and 1979.

Overwhelming evidence shows that heavy pesticide use in the U.S. and around the world has contributed to the environmental debt. It will eventually have to be paid in further human suffering and damage to the natural world.

Earthkeepers' Response

What can and should be done?

It is clear that further pesticide contamination of people, food, and water should be reduced as rapidly as possible. Individuals, churches, and community groups must become aware of the moral and ethical implications of pesticide contamination. They need to become active to influence governing bodies to more forcefully safeguard the environment.

Individuals can stop or severely restrict pesticide use. People can limit their purchases of fruits and vegetables produced with pesticides. Ellan Haas, executive director of Public Voice for Food and Health Policy, says, "Consumers should be wary of perfect-looking produce which was probably sprayed liberally with pesticides."

Richard Wiles, project officer for the National Academy of Sciences pesticides study, recommends that people carefully wash all produce. "We can't wash everything all off of anything but keep washing," he says. "Wash and write your congressperson."

Sandra Marquardt of the National Coalition Against Misuse of Pesticides says, "Consumers should buy organic produce when possible and write their representatives on both the state and federal levels."

The root cause of pesticide contamination is a misunderstanding of how the natural world really works. Use of pesticides promotes a control-of-nature mentality. It is true that nature's laws may be circumvented for a time. But nature knows best. Whatever is sowed will be reaped. The time for reaping the consequences of pesticide pollution is at hand. Are we willing to make the necessary changes in our living to minimize these consequences?

9. Toxic Waste Dumping on the Poor

The industrial nations of the world have a problem. Their industries are generating millions of tons of toxic waste that nobody wants in their backyards.

Scandals in which U.S. and European companies conspired with poor, debt-ridden African governments to dump toxic wastes in their countries have been reported widely by the world press. Recent studies document that toxic wastes are also being dumped beside poor communities of ethnic minorities in the United States. That also is a scandal. Is there a Christian perspective on these injustices?

Dumping on the Poor

A map of Africa in the August 1988 issue of *South* magazine highlights ten countries where toxic waste dumping has already occurred, is now operational, or is under review. The commentary states that "industrialized countries have been dumping toxic industrial and radioactive waste in developing countries for decades. . . . What has changed is that environmentalist groups have stepped up monitoring of toxic waste disposal methods and shipments, and curbs in industrial countries have been tightened."

One toxic dumping scandal occurred near the small port town of KoKo in Nigeria. Reporters found 3,800 tons of toxic waste in more than 2,000 drums, sacks, and containers on a farm there. The waste, shipped from Italy, contained 150 tons of polychlorinated biphenyls (PCBs)—one of the world's most toxic and highly carcinogenic wastes—and some radioactive wastes.

A Norwegian ship dumped 15,000 tons of toxic incinerator ash from Philadelphia, Pa., on Kassa Island off the coast of the West African country of Guinea. Dying trees on the island alerted observers to the dump sites. The Guinea government asked the Norwegian government to remove the waste. Norway complied, with no word about where they would take the ash next.

Pressure to dump toxic wastes in Africa and other parts of the Third World is intense. It is expensive for Western industries to dispose of toxic waste in their own countries—up to $2,500 per ton. So waste brokers look to countries where it costs less.

From Morocco to the Congo, virtually every country on West Africa's coast reported receiving offers in 1988 from American or European companies seeking cheap sites to dispose of hazardous waste, according to *The New York Times* (17 July 1988). The fees offered have been as low as $2.50 a ton.

The Rights of the Poor

The money that could be made is tempting, as the story of Nigerian farmer Sunday Nana illustrates. Ecomar Service, a waste management firm in Livorno, Italy, convinced Nana to store 2,500 tons of PCB waste on his land near KoKo for a service fee of $100 per month.

That likely seemed good to Nana. Per capita gross national product in Nigeria averages $767 per year. If the contract had run for five years, he would have received $6,000. Setting this against the fee Ecomar was charging the company to dispose of the waste, Ecomar stood to make U.S. $2.5 million on the deal, according to *South* magazine. Exposure of the scandal terminated the deal.

The government of Guinea-Bissau, in another deal, had a toxic waste contract for $40 a ton and hoped to make $120 million a year—more than its annual budget. The government changed its mind and canceled the contract when other toxic waste scandals became public.

Congo, too, expected to make a lot of money from toxic waste storage—then decided against it. Congolese information minister Christian-Gilbert Membet was quoted as saying the Congo "preferred to remain poor with honor."

Some toxic waste is dumped on America's poor. Charles Lee, director of research for the Commission for Racial Justice of the United Church of Christ, has studied the relationship between race and location of toxic waste dumps in the U.S. He has documented that a disproportionate number of such sites are located in communities where poor racial minorities live. Some of their commission findings include:

- The U.S. General Accounting Office studied the racial and socio-economic characteristics of communities surrounding toxic landfills in the Southeast. It found that three out of four communities were predominantly black and poor.
- America's largest toxic waste landfill, receiving waste from 45 states, is in largely black and poor Sumter County, Alabama.
- In Houston, Texas, six of the eight municipal incinerators and all five landfills are in poor, black neighborhoods.
- Forty percent of the nation's total commercial toxic waste landfill capacity is located in three predominantly black and Hispanic communities.

Lee quotes biologist Barry Commoner: "There is a functional link between racism, poverty, and powerlessness and the chemical industry's assault on the environment."

Dumping toxic wastes on God's earth, among poor people, is morally and ethically indefensible. The Bible is clear on the importance of properly tending the Lord's creation. Psalm 24:1 says, "The earth is the Lord's and all that is in it" (NEB).

The Bible is also clear about the need for Christians to care for and protect the poor. Proverbs 31:8-9 is typical: "Speak up for people who cannot speak for themselves. Protect the rights of all who are helpless. Speak for them and be a righteous judge. Protect the rights of the poor and needy" (TEV).

Earthkeepers' Response

What can Christians do about this injustice? We can consume less, recycle more, and use sparingly, if at all, materials such as pesticides and plastic foam cups that account for toxic waste. We can support groups like the Citizens Clearing House for Hazardous Waste, begun by Lois Gibbs of Love Canal fame. This group has many resources to help fight toxic waste dumping and work for alternatives. We can support local, national, and international legislation designed to prevent toxic waste production, its transport from place of origin, and its being dumped on the poor.

Under current U.S. law, toxic wastes can be shipped to a foreign country if the country is simply told about it and accepts it. The temptation of a poor country to accept toxic waste is too great. Shipping toxic waste usually moves it to nations without the technical ability to monitor its storage. Further, export removes the cost of managing wastes from consumers who benefited from the process that produced the waste, hiding the true environmental cost. Export of toxic waste should be prohibited.

Discussion Questions

1. It has been said (and practiced in the past) that "the solution to pollution is dilution." What does this mean? Why is this no longer an acceptable practice in many cases?

2. Who should pay for the cleanup of the 50,000 toxic waste dumps in America? Local, state, or federal governments? The companies (or individuals) who contributed to them? The next generation?

3. What should be done to prevent further toxic waste build-up? Where should toxic wastes be placed today when everyone wants to belong to the NIMBY (not in my backyard) Club?

4. Relate Christian lifestyle to the toxic waste issue.

5. The phrase "environmental debt" is used to discuss hazardous waste and other environmental degradation. Explain the phrase.

6. To what extent do you agree that "chemical contamination of our water supplies has become the most serious environmental problem of our time"?

7. Research the story of Love Canal. Evaluate its importance to the environmental movement.

8. Explain the "circle of poison."

9. Illustrate from the section on dumping hazardous waste in Africa why it is such a lucrative activity for the industrialized countries.

10. Evaluate the evidence given by Charles Lee that there are more toxic waste dumps located near minorities and/or the poor in the U.S.

Resources

Everyone's Back Yard. Quarterly newsletter by Citizen's Clearinghouse for Hazardous Waste, Inc. (CCHW), P.O. Box 926, Arlington, VA 22216. CCHW has many publications on the hazardous waste problem in the United States. Write or call 703 276-7070 for its listings.

For Our Children. A video and study guide produced by the United Methodists. Available from MCC, Akron, PA 17501.

King, Jonathan. *Troubled Water*. Emmaus, Pa.: Rodale Press, 1985. Several good chapters on toxic waste problems.

Norris, Ruth, and A. Karim Ahmed, eds. *Pills, Pesticides and Profits: The International Trade in Toxic Substances*. Croton-on-Hudson, N.Y.: North River Press, 1982.

Radioactive Waste Campaign. *Deadly Defense: Military Radioactive Landfills*. Second Floor, 625 Broadway, New York, NY 10012: Radioactive Waste Campaign, 1988. Well-documented information on all U.S. radioactive waste problems.

Shantilal. *What Does It Profit. . .?* Newsletter from The Brethren Press, 1983.

Void of Desolation, A. Friendship Press, 1985. A 16-minute filmstrip, available from MCC, Akron, PA 17501, or Church World Service film libraries in the U.S. Excellent presentation of toxic waste issues.

Weir, David, and Mark Shapiro. *Circle of Poison*. San Francisco: Institute for Food and Development Policy, 1981. Documents the global scandal of corporate and government exportation of pesticides.

Worldwatch Papers: *Altering the Earth's Chemistry* (Paper 71); *Reassessing Nuclear Power* (75); *Mining Urban Wastes* (76); and *Defusing the Toxics Threat* (79). Available from Worldwatch Institute, 1776 Mass. Ave. NW, Washington, DC 20036.

Wrath of Grapes. United Farm Workers, 1987. A 15-minute video cassette showing effects of pesticides on farm workers in California. From National Farm Worker Ministry, 111-A Fairmont Ave., Oakland, CA 94611.

Water Pollution

*Like cold water to a weary soul
is good news from a distant land.*
      —Proverbs 25:25

*Come, all you who are thirsty,
   come to the waters;
and you who have no money,
   come, buy and eat!*
      —Isaiah 55:1a

*We Americans are not accustomed to worrying about our water.
Undrinkable tap water is a problem that we associate with the
Third World. . . . But whether you drink chlorinated municipal
water or pump your own from a hand-dug 100-year-old well, the
era is past when you could take water for granted.*
      —Jonathan King in *Troubled Waters*

10. The U.S. Tap-Water Rebellion Is On

The great "tap-water rebellion" is on. More and more Americans are becoming concerned about the safety of their drinking water as they learn how vulnerable it is to contamination.

National legislators are beginning to heed the outcry of Americans worried about contaminated water and toxic waste dumps by belatedly addressing the cleanup issue. Unfortunately, Congress is doing little about pollution prevention.

On 21 January 1987, the U.S. Senate passed a $20-billion, updated Clean Water Act by a vote of 93 to 6. The House had passed the bill by a vote of 406 to 8 on January 8. The law passed over a presidential veto by Ronald Reagan.

The drought and the waste on the beaches in 1988 opened the eyes of the public to how we have been mistreating the earth. A five-year, $9-billion extension of the federal superfund bill was approved by Congress and signed by the president in 1988. It was a renewed effort to clean up thousands of toxic waste dump sites in the U.S., estimated to cost billions of dollars.

The Issues

Critical environmental issues are again being addressed, at least on the federal level. Sociologist Riley E. Dunlap, who follows public opinion on environmental issues, attributes the increase in public concern since 1980 to two factors: "(1) the realization by millions of Americans that hazardous wastes are a threat to their families' health, and (2) a growing distrust of the government's role in environmental protection. The public's assumption that everything was taken care of was destroyed by the Reagan Administration" (*Christian Science Monitor*, 14 January 1987).

A National Wildlife Federation poll of Americans released in the February-March 1987 edition of *National Wildlife* verifies Dunlap's first observation. Americans see the contamination of their drinking water as a serious concern. In the poll readers were asked: "What do you perceive as the greatest threat to your environment?"

Of eight environmental threats listed, 1,300 respondents chose these priorities:

1. Drinking water contamination
2. Leaking hazardous waste sites
3. Toxic gases in the air
4. Acid rain
5. Air pollution from automobiles
6. Water pollution from farm and city runoff
7. Nuclear energy
8. Indoor air pollution

Dunlap mentioned "distrust of the government's role in environmental protection." Evidence indicates clearly that the EPA has failed in its mission in recent years. Jonathan King reports in his 1985 book *Troubled Water*:

• The EPA is supposed to conduct research, set standards, and administer several complex environmental laws that regulate literally millions of sources of pollution that affect everybody living in this country. Clearly the agency doesn't have enough money to do its job.

• In more than 10 years since the Safe Drinking Water Act was passed, the EPA referred only 21 cases of violations for prosecution although thousands of violations occurred each year.

• [The Reagan Administration] tried its best to dismantle the

EPA when it took office in 1980. Over its first term, the budget for drinking water programs was cut 31 percent, hazardous waste programs were cut 16 percent, and money for pesticide regulations was reduced 32 percent.

• The EPA budget for scientific research and development was slashed by nearly 50 percent from 1980-1984. . . . Research is vital to the agency's regulatory decisions. It's difficult to set safe drinking water standards without knowing whether or not a chemical causes cancer or birth defects.

Endangered Drinking Water

The tap-water rebellion is a welcome development. We hope it is not too late. According to the *National Wildlife's* nineteenth annual Environmental Quality Index (E-Q Index), water pollution in the United States continues to be an urgent problem. The reasons are apparent:

• One out of two U.S. citizens uses groundwater as her or his source of drinking water.

• A survey conducted by state water officials found that nearly one out of every four miles of U.S. rivers and one out of every five lakes are being spoiled or threatened by pollutants from farms, mines, and urban areas.

• In California, 20 percent of the state's largest drinking water wells are contaminated at levels above legal safety limits. In Iowa, authorities detected pesticides in at least half the state's city wells.

• According to U.S. and Canadian researchers, the 37 million people who live around the Great Lakes generally have 20 percent higher levels of toxic chemicals in their bodies than other North Americans due to contaminated fish and drinking water.

• The EPA estimates that more than one-third of the country's 800,000 underground storage tanks are leaking toxic substances into groundwater.

One basic type of water pollution is that caused by discharge of untreated or inadequately treated wastewater into rivers, lakes, and reservoirs. This is known as point source pollution and generally can be controlled by wastewater treatment. Developed countries are aware of this kind of water pollution and are attempting to control it. A 1985 study done by the Organization for Economic Cooperation and Development (OECD) documents the percentage of population in each country served by such wastewater treatment plants from 1970 to 1983. The results charted in *World Resources 1986* (p. 135) show that Sweden has now reached its goal of 100 percent of its population so served. The U.S. has remained at about 65 percent, while Spain and Belgium have only 20 percent of their population served by treatment plants.

The U.S., as well as most industrialized countries, has a long way to go to treat wastewater adequately for all the population. The newly passed clean water bill will provide $18 billion through 1994 to help states build more wastewater and sewage treatment plants.

Another type of water quality problem is the increasing eutrophication of rivers and lakes despite wastewater treatment. This type of pollution from large areas (called nonpoint sources) is mainly caused by runoff of pesticides, herbicides, and fertilizers from agricultural lands. These chemicals enrich the water excessively, causing tiny algae plants to thrive with consequent oxygen depletion upon their death, leading to a "dead" lake.

One of the worst forms of groundwater pollution facing the U.S. today is nitrate contamination. The main source of nitrates in groundwater is nitrogen-based fertilizer that leaches through the soil into the water table. Another source is animal waste leachment. According to King, more than 500,000 households in the U.S. are drinking water that contains potentially unsafe levels of nitrates. While the adult health risks of nitrates are still being studied, it is known that high levels of nitrates can cause oxygen depletion in infants. In adults, once ingested, nitrates may be converted to cancer-causing chemicals—possibly related to stomach cancer.

Pesticide pollution of groundwater is also increasing in the U.S. King quotes Dr. Christopher Wilkinson, EPA scientific advisory panel member, as saying, "Groundwater contamination by pesticides and/or pesticides residues is probably the single biggest environmental issue of the next decade." The U.S. Department of Agriculture estimates that 2.5 billion pounds of pesticides are applied annually to American soil, an 1,800-percent increase since 1947.

Earthkeepers' Response

What is an appropriate response to the increasing pollution of our water resources today?

First, we must individually and collectively pay for our past neglect. We must support local, state, and national efforts to clean up pollution. This will be costly. The EPA estimates that it will take $108 billion through the year 2000 just to provide the U.S. with enough wastewater and sewage treatment plants. The Clean Water Act of 1987 is to provide only $18 billion through 1994 for the above purpose.

Second, and most important, we need to stop pollution at its source. Do we really need 600,000 chemicals to provide quality living today? It's clear that these chemicals are the main cause of the present dilemma. To stop polluting our water sources, we will need to radically change our lifestyles. We must move away from farming with inorganic fertilizers, pesticides, and herbicides. We must stop chemical lawn and golf course care, vegetable and fruit spraying. Calls for changes to protect groundwater have increasing popular support, yet companies producing and marketing these chemicals are resisting major reductions. Part of the challenge is to make clear the real costs of continued chemical use and abuse.

Discussion Questions

1. Relate widespread pesticide use to water pollution in the U.S. What has already happened and what is the risk potential?

2. What evidence is there that groundwater pollution is becoming a serious problem in the U.S.? How can water pollution be reversed?

3. Pesticides, toxic waste, and water pollution are related. Point out some of these connections.

4. Of the many actions listed that can prevent water pollution, which are ones you can and will do? Be specific.

5. Explain eutrophication. Why does it occur? What are the consequences of the process?

6. Have you had your drinking water tested for chemical residues? Is this an essential activity today?

Resources

King, Jonathan. *Troubled Water*. Emmaus, Pa.: Rodale Press, 1985. Several good chapters on toxic waste problems.

Norris, Ruth, ed. *Pills, Pesticides and Profits*. New York: North River Press, 1982. Discusses the circle of poison.

Postle, Sandra. *Water: Rethinking Management in an Age of Scarcity* (Worldwatch Paper 62); and *Conserving Water: The Untapped Alternative* (67). Available from Worldwatch Institute, 1776 Mass. Ave. NW, Washington, DC 20036.

World Commission on Environment and Development, The. *Our Common Future*. New York: Oxford Press, 1987. Chapter 10, "Managing The Commons," has good information on water pollution.

Soil Erosion

The Lord God took the man and put him in the Garden of Eden to work it and take care of it.
    —Genesis 2:15

Civilization can survive the exhaustion of oil reserves, but not the continuing wholesale loss of topsoil.
    —Lester R. Brown in *Building a Sustainable Society*

11. Save the Family Farm to Save the Soil

Why save the family farm? There are many good reasons, but perhaps the most important is that this is the best way to combat soil erosion and environmental destruction in farming areas. There is much evidence that the traditional family farm is best equipped to practice soil conservation. It is worth every effort to save the family farm for this reason alone.

What is a family farm? In *The Family Farm: Can It Be Saved?* Shantilal P. Bhagat gives a good description: "The family farm is an economic unit whose labor requirement is no larger than what can be supplied by the family that resides on it."

The farm family is seen as somewhat conservative, placing high value on the family and the land. Traditional values inculcated by family farms include good work habits, family unity, simplicity, honesty, and self-reliance.

Down the River

Both family farms and their topsoil are being lost to a dramatic degree today. The Conservation Foundation reported in 1988 that for every pound of food produced in the U.S., 22 pounds of soil erodes. The U.S. Department of Agriculture (USDA) states that "loss of soil through erosion exceeds tolerable levels on 44 percent of U.S. cropland."

Anson R. Bertrand of the USDA describes soil erosion in the U.S. as having reached epidemic proportions. Abundant data illustrate the loss of family farms in the United States and subsequent changes:

- In 1935, there were 6.8 million farms; in 1988, there were fewer than 2.2 million. An average of 30,000 farms have gone out of business annually since 1970.
- In 1929, 30 percent of the U.S. population resided on family farms; today that figure is 2.4 percent.
- The average U.S. farm size is about 430 acres.
- Ownership of farmland has become highly concentrated. A mere one percent of farmland owners control more than 30 percent of the total acreage. In 1982, 1.5 percent of U.S. farms (those netting $500,000 or more annually) received about 90 percent of all net farm income.
- In 1988, 35 percent of all U.S. farmland was owned by nonfarmers, 40 percent was rented, and 10 percent was held by corporations.

Some U.S. farmland is held by insurance companies and the amount is increasing as family farmers go bankrupt. The Land Stewardship Project (LSP), a Minnesota-based land ethics group, claims that John Hancock Insurance owns 222,000 acres of farm and timberland in the United States. This is an area one-third the size of Rhode Island.

Down the Drain

A dramatic example of the relationship between the loss of a family farm and environmental degradation is reported by the LSP. In 1958, Ed Hauck of Wabasha County, Minnesota, bought a dairy farm. He put in soil conservation measures, including terraces, hay strips, waterways, and contours. By 1984 he had developed his farm into an award-winning conservation showplace. Soil erosion had been cut to less than three tons per acre, according to the Wabasha County Soil Conservation Service.

In January 1985, Hauck was a victim of foreclosure. An insurance company took over the farm and rented it out to a cash grain farmer who plowed it up fence row to fence row, removing all terraces, waterways, strips, and contours. Twenty-seven years of conservation work went down the drain. The Soil Conservation Service predicts an annual soil loss of 34 to 40 tons per acre per year—a tenfold increase.

LSP claims the Hauck farm tragedy is not an isolated one. They point to similar cases in Missouri, Iowa, Nebraska, and Wisconsin. More and more farmland is being taken over by groups more interested in immediate dollar profit than in long-term protection of soil and the environment.

Earthkeepers' Response

The LSP motto is: "Let's stop treating our soil like dirt."
Amen.

12. Soil Erosion: Quiet Crisis in the World Economy

In 1984 Lester R. Brown and Edward C. Wolf, in Worldwatch Paper 60, labeled soil erosion as the "quiet crisis." They point out that increasing world population and other demands have put great pressure on farmers to produce more food. And produce they have. World food output has more than doubled over the past generation, but this has come at the high price of excessive soil erosion.

Some soil erosion is natural, but today it far exceeds natural soil formation. As the demand for food climbs, the world is beginning to "mine" its soils, converting a renewable resource into a nonrenewable one.

Loss of topsoil has been a quiet crisis. Nowhere has the depletion of topsoil gained the attention paid to the depletion of oil reserves, for example. Governments have responded to the oil crisis. The critical but more subtle soil erosion problem has not been addressed sufficiently.

Brown and Wolf estimate there will be a sharp reduction in the amount of cropland topsoil available worldwide by the year 2000. They also project a 19-percent decline in cropland per person between 1984 and 2000. The amount of topsoil per person, assuming current rates of soil erosion, shows a 32-percent decline in the same period.

Causes of Soil Erosion

Soil erosion is caused by many factors, including:

• The pressure of economic incentives on farmers to produce more.

• Competition for cropland, forcing farmers to use land not suited for cultivation.

• Increasing population pressure, especially in the Third World.

• Abandoning crop rotation and other sustainable types of agriculture.

• Rising demand for food that reduces the area fallowed in key dryland farming regions. This leads to wind erosion.

• Shortened fallowing and rotation cycles in tropical regions due to population pressure. Organic content and thus water-holding capacity is reduced with subsequent soil erosion.

• The shift to large-scale equipment and farming in developed countries such as the U.S.

A study on cropping systems and soil erosion shows how erosion is increased by abandoning rotation and planting the same crop year after year.

Cropping system	*Average annual soil loss per acre*
Corn, wheat, and clover rotation	2.7 tons
Continuous wheat	10.1 tons
Continuous corn	19.7 tons

Much of the decline in real soil fertility that occurs with topsoil loss due to row crop cultivation is being masked by artificial synthetic inputs, particularly by the increasing use of fertilizer (Worldwatch Paper 60, page 11).

How Bad Is It?

Soil erosion is serious. A 1968 study by geologist Sheldon Judson estimated that river-borne soil sediment carried into the oceans was 9 billion tons per year before the introduction of modern agricultural practices. Now it is about 24 billion tons per year.

The most recent figures on river sediment flow show the world's rivers carrying heavy loads of soil to the oceans. Scientists have recently documented that vast amounts of wind-borne soil are also being deposited in the oceans.

Reports from the U.S.S.R. indicate that topsoil erosion is at least as great there as in North America. It is clear that the Soviet Union has had food production problems in recent years. Pressure to decrease the nation's need for imported food focuses on agriculture and, as in North America, contributes to land use practices that increase soil erosion.

The erosion rate for China, the world's fourth major food-producing country, and India are estimated at greater than twice that of the U.S. Given the pressure on land in the Third World for food production, a conservative assumption would be that its soil loss rate overall would be at least similar to those above.

The authors calculate from their data that the average depth of remaining topsoil worldwide is about seven inches. It is being depleted at about 0.7 percent per year or 7 percent per decade. As soil is lost, productivity decreases. One study reported that for each centimeter-thick layer of topsoil lost through water erosion, corn yield was reduced by 2.34 bushels per acre, or about six bushels for each inch of topsoil lost.

Costs of Erosion

Tables from other studies show the effect of topsoil loss on corn and wheat yields. They clearly verify the loss of productivity.

Other experiments lead to the demand to compensate for soil loss with increased chemical fertilizer application.

The costs of erosion are not confined to the farm alone. Eroded soil may end up on local streams, rivers, canals, or irrigation and hydroelectric reservoirs. There it may interfere with irrigation, navigability of waterways, or electrical generation. For example, one reservoir in Pakistan is projected to fill with silt 25 years earlier than originally planned because of excessive erosion.

A rather dramatic indirect cost of erosion is the projected loss of navigability of the Panama Canal. There is deforestation and the plowing of steeply sloping land in the watershed area by landless farmers. This combination is leading to an unprecedented siltation of the lakes that make up part of the canal. If the trend continues, the canal's capacity to handle shipping will be greatly reduced by the end of the century.

Soil erosion control will be extremely costly. Studies show that soil erosion control is not economical in the short term, based strictly on dollars and cents. One Iowa study suggests that short-term costs to farmers would be three times as great as benefits.

The economics of erosion control in the North America have recently become more attractive using new no-till or conservation tillage practices. The share of harvested cropland in conservation tillage rose from 10 percent in 1972 to 33 percent in 1984. No-till farming is a hopeful step in the right direction for economical control of erosion. But the environmental impact of the chemicals needed for the practice must also be a consideration.

Government involvement will be crucial to bring erosion under control because:

- Farmers alone in the short term can't afford the practices needed to reduce erosion.
- Only the government can calculate the long-term aggregate cost of soil erosion, including the off-farm costs mentioned before.
- Governments are best equipped to gather the information needed on the relationship between soil erosion and land productivity.

Mobilizing public support for adequately funded soil conservation programs will require extensive public education on the problem. Scientific proof of the necessity of soil conservation is not sufficient. National political leaders must be involved. Political will grounded in awareness is often the missing ingredient needed to act on conservation measures.

Food Deficits

Over the past generation, many countries developed food deficits, but few link the shortages with the depletion of their soil by erosion. In these countries people know that food prices are rising, but most don't know why. An understanding that lost soil now means costlier food for years to come is needed to galvanize support for a public soil conservation ethic.

Global economics is also an important factor. As world food demand has begun its second doubling since midcentury, pressures on land have become so intense that close to half the world's cropland is losing topsoil at a rate undermining its long-term productivity. Agriculture is the foundation of the global economy. This loss of topsoil, if not reversed, will undermine the economy itself. Few countries are responding effectively to this emerging threat.

The media describes widening food deficits, chronic hunger, and a world in economic trouble. Eager to maximize food output today, we borrow from tomorrow. The permanent loss of over 25 billion tons of topsoil from our croplands each year is the price we pay for shortsighted agricultural policies designed to boost food output at the expense of soils.

Soil erosion will lead to higher food prices, hunger, and probably persistent pockets of famine. The world has weathered a severalfold increase in the price of oil over the past decade. But it is not well equipped to cope with even modest rises in the price of food. Although the immediate effects of soil erosion are economic, the ultimate effects are social.

Earthkeepers' Response

The world is faring poorly in developing model efforts to conserve soil. There are few national successes, few examples other countries can emulate. Historically, soil erosion has been a local problem. In the late twentieth century, food, like oil, is a global commodity. The excessive loss of topsoil anywhere ultimately affects food prices everywhere. The causes of erosion listed above can give us clues on how to retard loss of soil and enhance natural soil formation.

Discussion Questions

1. Review the causes of soil erosion. How can it be prevented?

2. In the short term, it is economically more costly to practice soil conservation in agriculture. Who should pay these costs?

3. It is usually said that the traditional family farmer practices better soil conservation. (Better than whom?) Do you agree? What evidence substantiates your answer?

4. What does it mean to "mine" the soil? What's wrong with mining the soil?

5. Does a biblical view of the land motivate farmers to practice good soil conservation? Do Christians treat their land better than non-Christians?

6. What responsibility do each of these groups have to save the family farm: Governments (federal, state, local)? Farm organizations? Individuals? The church? Other groups?

7. What methods of soil conservation have been most effective in your experience? Evaluate the pros and cons of methods observed or experienced.

Resources

Brown, Lester R., ed. *State of the World 1987*. Washington, D.C.: Worldwatch Institute, 1987. Chapter 7 deals with soil erosion and other agricultural issues.

Brown, Lester R., and Edward Wolf. *Soil Erosion: Quiet Crisis in the World Economy*. Worldwatch Paper 60, Sept. 1984. Worldwatch Institute, 1776 Mass. Ave. NW, Washington, DC 20036.

Down on the Farm: Examining Agriculture's Twin Dilemmas, Land and Profit. NOVA-produced 55-minute video cassette available for free rental from Center for Rural Affairs, Box 405, Walthill, NE 68067. Excellent piece dealing with regional impact of soil erosion and pesticide use.

Freudenberger, C. Dean. *Food for Tomorrow?* Minneapolis: Augsburg Press, 1984. Good chapters on soil erosion and related issues, written by an agronomist-theologian.

Gift of Land, The. Teleketics, 1982. Two 15-minute filmstrips in a series of five deal with soil erosion: *A Broken Covenant: A Broken Land;* and *How Land Abuse Happens.* Both filmstrips available from MCC, Akron, PA 17501.

Platt, LaVonne G., ed. *Hope for the Family Farm.* Newton, Kan.: Faith and Life Press, 1987. Chapter on agriculture sustainability discusses soil erosion.

Strip-Mining

The earth is defiled by its people;
*   they have disobeyed the laws,*
violated the statues
*   and broken the everlasting covenant.*
Therefore a curse consumes the earth.
        —Isaiah 24:5-6a

I conceive a strip-miner to be a model exploiter. . . . The exploiter is
a specialist, an expert. . . . The standard of the exploiter is
efficiency. . . . The exploiter's goal is money, profit. . . . The
exploiter asks of a piece of land only how much and how quickly it
can be made to produce.
        —Wendell Berry in *The Unsettling of America*

13. Strip-Mining: The Earth Defiled

The loss and deterioration of cropland means an increasingly hungry world. Severe pressure is being placed on the world's arable land by urbanization, industrialization, surface mining, soil erosion, desertification, and other human activities. Even land in its natural state is worth respecting; it is not there to be exploited for short-term profit. Surface mining contributes to this land loss and degradation.

More surface mining (48 percent) is done to obtain coal than anything else. Sand, gravel, stone, phosphate rock, clay, copper, iron ore, and uranium are mined in the same way. This process, often called strip-mining, simply involves removing overburden (topsoil and subsoil) above a resource and mechanically removing the raw materials. The soil then may or may not be replaced, depending on the interests of the mining enterprise. Unless great care is taken to keep topsoil segregated from subsoil, even returned soils may be of negligible fertility.

Moonscape on Earth

Art well remembers his first visit to strip-mined coal lands in east-central Ohio in 1958. On a field trip with a college class studying the conservation of natural resources, he was astonished by the devastation of the beautiful rolling land. There were thousands of acres of gorges, gullies, high walls, acid lakes, and mine spoils—all barren as the moonscape. In those days, reclamation laws, such as they were, called for clump-planting of hardy trees like black locust, sweet gum, silver maple, and pine on the devastated land. Leveling was not required. In many places few trees or other vegetation survived.

It will take hundreds of years for nature to restore the land to even modest productivity here. Several scientists were supposed to determine how to help nature out. They found few answers. In strip-mining, it is simpler to prevent damage than to repair it. To stem this land devastation, a group of interested people convinced the U.S. Congress to pass Public Law 95-87—The Surface Mining and Reclamation Act of 1977. It was a step in the right direction.

Little did Art think on that field trip in 1958 that we would have an opportunity later to work on reclaiming some of that "prelaw," degraded mine land. In 1973 we purchased a run-down, 80-acre farm in east-central Ohio near that 1958 field-trip site. About 35 acres of that farm was strip-mined from 1952 to 1955, clump-planted, and abandoned. We now had the challenge to help reclaim that 35 acres (as told in the next chapter).

How Bad Is It?

The amount of disturbed strip-mined land boggles the mind. A U.S. Department of the Interior study, released in 1982, found that nearly 6 million acres of land had been surface mined in the U.S. between 1930 and 1980. Six million acres is more than the combined land area of Connecticut, Delaware, and Rhode Island. It is more area than all the U.S. airport space, more than all U.S. railroad right-of-way, and one-third of all highway right-of-way. Only 47.4 percent of this disturbed land was reclaimed by 1980.

In Kentucky, Pennsylvania, Ohio, and West Virginia, more than 2 percent of the total land area is damaged by surface mining. In Illinois and Indiana, more than one percent of the land is disturbed. Most of this land was rich, productive forest or reasonably good cropland. In Illinois, a state with some of the most productive soil in the U.S., 202,422 acres in 40 counties have already been affected. Given the extensive resources of coal close to the surface in some 51 Illinois counties, the potential for more cropland disruption there is great.

It appears likely that surface mining, especially of coal, will increase. A 1983 U.S. Department of Energy Fact Sheet reported that 53.2 percent of electricity produced in 1982 was from coal. The amount of coal used to produce electricity was increasing at an average annual rate of 4.8 percent in the ten years following 1973. Petroleum and natural gas supplies are rapidly decreasing. The use of coal, of which there is a much larger supply, will increase to take up the slack. Surface mining is less costly and less hazardous than deep mining. Hence, pressure will increase to expand strip-mining operations.

Reclaiming Strip-mined Land

Some say that strip-mined land can be adequately reclaimed with modern techniques. But it is doubtful that it can really be made agriculturally productive again in the foreseeable future.

Subsurface water patterns are disturbed in the mining process. Water percolation suffers. Rock strata and minerals are rearranged. In some places iron pyrite is exposed and acid is formed. Acid drainage into rivers and lakes is a problem. A U.S. Department of Agriculture study concludes, "Surface mining as practiced in much of the nation today either ruins farmland completely or reduces its productivity drastically."

Most reclaimed land today can support only grassland or forest. Field crops generally do not do well. In southeastern Ohio, once 97 percent forested, the reclaimed rolling land is covered with sparse grass. It will take years for native forest to become reestablished.

What about reclaiming the thousands of acres of surface-mined land disturbed before 1977? Ohio has more than 200,000 such acres, Pennsylvania 300,000. Costs to reclaim this land are estimated between $10,000 and $14,000 per acre. At that rate it would take $2 billion to restore Pennsylvania's pre-law land alone. But only $82 million is available for the next 15 years. This money comes from a tax placed on present mining operations via Public Law 95-87. Obviously it will be a long time until all Pennsylvania land is reclaimed.

Most pre-law disturbed land is still in the hands of the coal companies who damaged it. They are apparently benefiting by leasing it and drilling for oil and gas. In some places they may plan to mine deeper veins of coal. They have little interest in restoring the land for crops or forests. Their original purpose for mining was profit. It still is.

Earthkeepers' Response

The dilemma of surface mining of coal continues. It is clear that we will need both cropland and energy to support future human population. Today there is roughly one acre of cropland per person worldwide. By the year 2050 it is estimated that figure will be less than 0.5 acre per person—0.24 acre in the developing world.

The energy from coal will be needed in the transition from fossil fuels to renewable forms of energy.

We can clearly see the relationships between electrical energy consumption, degradation of land by strip-mining, air pollution, and acid rain. Demand for more electricity at reasonable cost drives the strip-mining for coal, which despoils the land. Burning the coal to run generators produces air pollution and acid rain. The problems are obvious.

If we are serious about responsible stewardship of the Lord's earth and have compassion for future generations, we must reduce our consumption of energy from fossil fuels, develop alternate renewable types of energy, and restore lands already degraded. This is the way to resolve the dilemma and the way to renew the covenant that was to last forever, described in Isaiah 24.

14. Our Own Story of Land Reclamation

"Eighty acres, some wooded, log barn, year-round spring, house needs some work, remote" was the realtor's listing. After three years of searching for acreage, this sounded ideal. We knew ads could be deceiving. A house that needed "some work" was probably in need of major renovation, hardly habitable for humans.

As soon as possible after receiving the listing, Art drove 100 miles after school to see the 80 "remote" acres. It was a rainy evening in early June 1973 as he and the realtor walked through already tall vegetation. The realtor mentioned there were other people interested in the property. The owner was eager to sell. While discussing the details of a possible sale at a nearby truck stop, Art felt strongly that this property had good potential. It met the criteria we had set up several years earlier when we began looking for a piece of land.

We wanted at least 20 acres with a building or two within a two-hour drive of our home in the greater Cleveland, Ohio, area and costing no more than $10,000. Art took the next step as he signed the intent to purchase and bound the contract with all the money he had in his wallet that night—five dollars.

On his return home he announced with some trepidation what had transpired. Usually we conferred before making such major decisions. Within a week we and our three children visited the property and enthusiastically agreed with his choice.

Back to the Farm

Our original intent was to have a piece of land for our personal camping and retreat experiences—a place where we could read, write, and rock when we wanted to and had time. This land in the country would also provide a place to invite church friends to share in the peace of nature. Urban biology teachers and students could come to observe the creation firsthand.

During our years in the city we had spent many hours in the local park system, the Emerald Necklace, in all seasons of the year. We had camped in state and national parks, hiking and breathing the fresh air; we had backpacked in wilderness areas as a family for 10 years. This partially made up for the lack of outdoor experiences and communion with the creation that had naturally been a part of daily life in our own farm upbringings.

Both of us had grown up on diversified family farms in Ohio Mennonite communities with most of our aunts, uncles, and cousins living nearby. After graduating from high school, we attended Goshen (Indiana) College, where we met. Art majored in biology and Jocele in home economics, both graduating with teaching degrees. Our first teaching jobs were in farming communities in rural Ohio.

Our three children, two sons and a daughter, were born in small towns. Jocele opted to stay at home and assume the primary parenting role while the children were young. She soon became involved in church and community work that provided opportunities for personal growth and service to others. Art pursued graduate studies in science teaching. When offered a position in a suburban Cleveland high school, he accepted the challenge and the family moved to Ohio's largest metropolitan area. One of the highlights of the 23 years there was worshiping and fellowshipping with a racially integrated congregation. We enjoyed the cultural advantages and the excitement of living in the urban setting, but we also wanted to stay in touch with natural settings.

Further investigation of the 80 acres revealed a variety of landscapes ranging from dense woods to barren strip-mined spoil banks, from serene pasture land to ravines. Much of the farm was then an overgrown jungle of vegetation. Hidden under the greenery were mounds of cans, broken bottles, decaying buildings, and assorted building materials from a tenant who had been a roofer. Previous residents had left worn-out car bodies. We dubbed the property a walk-in garbage can.

Cleanup and Tree Planting

The first activities were to clean up and cut grass and plants growing around the house. Truckloads of scrap metal were hauled off to the recycler. As we cleared the overgrowth, flowering annuals, fruit trees, berry bushes, wildflowers, and a variety of native trees emerged. We then turned our labors to the house, which had been vandalized and then inhabited by roaming dogs and nesting birds. Our children and their friends soon took ownership in the project. "The farm" became a favorite weekend and vacation spot.

Early gardening attempts were productive. Art fulfilled his lifelong dream of planting several thousand strawberry plants. We planted 50 fruit trees, and the young orchard is now beginning to produce. We have added blueberries, raspberries, grapes, asparagus, and rhubarb. These supply food for our table, to share with acquaintances, and occasionally to sell at nearby fresh produce markets.

The remnants of the '50s strip-mining, gray piles of subsoil resembling moonscapes, were harder to repair. About 35 of the 80 acres had been strip-mined and were not reclaimed. We began to research ways to reclaim degraded strip-mined land. We learned the least expensive first step was to plant trees on the barren stripped areas. The land denuded by strip-mining began to respond well to plantings of coniferous trees.

During the first 15 years we have planted 12,000 trees, subsidized by the Ohio Department of Natural Resources (ODNR). Family members and friends helped plant the trees by hand. About 75 to 80 percent of the trees are growing. Some planted 15 years ago are now 40 feet tall. Pine needles falling to the ground build up duff, rebuilding the soil. Deciduous tree seedlings are taking root. Brambles and other green plants are filling in the bare spots under the trees. Vegetation in some of the wooded areas is now so thick as to be impassable.

Acid runoff has been decreased so that a greater variety of plants can grow, and a lake left by the mining operation is less acid. We have dubbed this the "red lake" from the color of the iron compounds. As it becomes less acid, its color is clearer. We hope it will eventually support a normal community of plant and animal life.

About 20 strip-mined acres are now supporting plant life through clump planting by the miners, our plantings, and the natural growth of plant life. Fifteen acres remain to be reclaimed. We have contacted government agencies for financial help to reclaim the worst areas. The cost to properly reclaim this type of stripped land through leveling and replanting is $10,000 to $14,000 per acre.

When Public Law 95-87 was passed in 1977, we applied for cost-share funds to assist in reclamation of about 20 acres of severely degraded gorges, high walls, and mine spoils on our land. The government inspection team placed our severely damaged land in the "least hazardous" category. "Most hazardous" lands are located adjacent to population centers. There acid water from streams drains into existing water supplies, or high walls and lakes pose safety hazards to nearby residents. There was no assistance available for us. So much for the new law! Without help, that acreage will remain in a state of degradation for many years.

In the spring of 1989, ODNR crews planted trees on a 260-acre plot that includes our land. Although the agency does not have the budget to level the high walls and fill in the gorges, the planting is a step in the right direction. It will certainly improve the appearance and hasten restoration of the land to a semblance of its former productivity.

Partnership Farming

Improvements continued as we dreamed and worked with the land. There were always more goals than we could achieve. Hiking trails were marked and trimmed to provide access to the wild areas. One section of wooded area was fenced from cattle and is returning to native oak, hickory, and beech forest. Cattle graze the pasture areas. Chickens in varying numbers are kept for meat and eggs. The animal manure provides fertilizer for the vegetable garden and orchard. An all-weather spring was developed to provide running water in the house and fresh water for the animals.

A few years after we bought the farm, our son and daughter-in-law asked to live in the farmhouse for a year between jobs. They stayed for nine years. Other families saw the relatively simple lifestyle they were able to maintain, growing much of their own food while beginning a graphic arts business.

They began to talk about additional land so that they, too, could have their own land to grow food, harvest firewood, and enjoy a life nearer to God's creation. Land prices were escalating at this time. Sixty-five acres half a mile away became available at what we thought an exorbitant price. Our modest offer, using the appreciated value of our farm land as collateral, was accepted.

With more land now available, there were more families interested. Our initial plan had been to subdivide the land into five-acre plots. Each piece would include a spot for a house with good orientation to the sun for most efficient solar gain, a fertile garden plot, and a woodland for fuel. A loop road, a good well, and a pond had already been developed on the land.

Then we ran into a problem. There was not adequate road frontage for each property. Our county has few building restrictions, but the requirements for roads for housing developments are similar to those in urban areas. Building a road to meet this code would have escalated the cost of each lot beyond the reach of those interested. Rather than petition for a variance, we went the route of a land trust, where the land is owned in a partnership. This concept fit the ideals of many in the group who wanted to hold the land in such a way that it is respected and not "owned" nor used only to make profit.

Since land trusts are relatively uncommon, we did a lot of research to set up the procedure and agreement. We received help from an interested Christian attorney who encouraged us to pioneer in this area. The Deer Spring Partners Land Trust was born and the first family—our older son, his wife, and two young children—built a home in 1980. Today there are eight homes completed and another in process.

The homes are small. Concern for environmental responsibility is uppermost. We used local materials such as rough-sawn tulip poplar for siding and oak beams from trees in the woodland. Several of the early homes used bricks from a local factory for floors. These provide the heat bank of the heating system. Building plans are submitted for group counsel.

There was desire for a community where people would share as intentional neighbors, but not go the full route of an intentional community where all property and income are held in common.

We drew up an agreement that covered legal matters and provided for community concerns. This agreement has been revised in its 10 years of existence and is open to constant study as the group defines its parameters. (Copies of the agreement are available from the authors of this book.)

The members of the group have spent many hours making decisions about their lives together. This group process is a deliberate one, requiring time and effort from the partners. It is also satisfying as consensus is reached and as the community develops among the member households.

Faith and Lifestyle

When four couples located in the community, they began a house church. They were all of Mennonite background and lived 45 minutes from the nearest Mennonite congregation. When the group outgrew their homes, it rented a hall for meeting. Currently this group has joined the Ohio Conference of the Mennonite Church and shares meeting space with a small Methodist congregation in the area. About 45 people meet regularly. Half of them are children, 12 and under.

It has always been the desire of the group to contribute to the community. This is a rural area on the fringe of Appalachia. The economy is based on agriculture, industry, and coal mining. The latter is mostly strip-mining of soft, high-sulfur coal. There are many oil and gas wells in the area. These are poor quality compared with high-quality mid-East oil. Many are capped, waiting for higher prices. Several factories have moved into the county, drawing on the low property tax base and potential labor pool. Health workers, social workers, and school teachers from the Deer Spring community are well respected in their service professions.

The beauty of the hills and river valleys in all seasons makes this an attractive area. The local hill folk are hard working and morally upstanding. Ohio's urban centers are within a two-hour drive west or north. For us this is an ideal place to research and write about world issues. We spend a part of the time working as stewards of the earth as we garden and observe God's creation.

The area is rich with history of the Native Americans. Set apart in this fashion, we must rethink and establish our own standards of economic and ecologic living. Being within a community of people with similar ideals provides a support group to help us carry out this way of life with integrity.

With the opportunity for Art to take early retirement in 1981, we felt ready for new challenges with Mennonite Central Committee (MCC), the relief and service agency of Mennonite and Brethren in Christ churches. This led to a year in Grenada and three years in the development education office at MCC headquarters in Akron, Pennsylvania. But we had projects still to complete on our land and a desire to strengthen family relationships with aging parents, children, and grandchildren. Therefore, we returned to the land in Ohio, where we work half-time for MCC and continue with land-related concerns. This gives credibility to our concerns about the environment. We can work to implement wise use of land, air, and water as we share challenges through writing and speaking.

In 1985 one of our sons, who lived in the farmhouse with his family, built a two-story, energy-efficient house for us near the red lake bordering the orchard. He, along with family members and friends, did considerable research on such homes. Some acquaintances had incorporated energy-efficient components in their houses. A south-facing slope on the edge of a wooded area was selected as the building site. Concrete walls were poured as the north, east, and west foundation walls of the 24-by-30-foot structure. These thick walls were insulated and waterproofed on the outside. Sand under the poured concrete lower level floor plus the thick concrete walls serve as a "heat sink" for collected solar energy. Large thermal glass windows on the lower level admit sunlight far back into the house during the winter, when the sun is low in the sky. An overhang blocks the sun in the summer, helped by shade trees. The highly insulated house is warm in winter and cool in summer.

We heat with a small Swedish wood stove, burning less than two cords of wood each year. There are several baseboard electric heaters for backup heat when we are away from home in the winter. We would like to supplement electricity with a wind generator or photovoltaic power in the future.

Local rough-sawn tulip or yellow poplar was used for the board-and-batten siding. Energy-efficient windows, six inches of insulation in the side walls, and heavy insulation in the attic complete the energy features.

From our house we can see into the adjacent woods. We enjoy watching the wildlife—a variety of birds, deer, squirrels, and wild turkeys.

Discussion Questions

1. Why does it take so long for U.S. land that was surface mined before 1977 to recover?

2. Do you think it is better to get energy for electricity from coal-fired plants or nuclear generators, or from renewable energy sources such as the wind, water, and sun? Evaluate the advantages and disadvantages.

3. The Bible states that God gave humans dominion over the creation. Do you think this includes the right to surface mine? Why or why not?

4. Since 1930, over 6 million acres have been degraded by surface mining. Only about half of that land has been reclaimed. How important is it to reclaim that land? Why? Who should do it? From where should the money come?

5. From cumulative budget deficits the United States has an incredible federal debt of about $3 trillion in 1990. It also has built up a vast environmental deficit from land degradation caused by soil erosion, water and air pollution, and toxic wastes. Which may be more significant in the long run? Discuss this second deficit. How did it come to be? How can it be reduced? What is Christian responsibility for this?

6. Do you know of individuals or communities attempting to live in a more responsible way ecologically? To what degree have they been successful? Evaluate.

7. How important is it for Christians to have community support in living out ecological principles in today's world? Explain.

Resources

Mitchell, John G. "The Mountains, the Miners, and the Mister Caudill." *Audubon Magazine*. November 1988. Article on Kentucky lawyer Harry Caudill's fight with King Coal.

Squillace, Mark. *Stripmining Handbook*. Washington, D.C.: Environmental Policy Institute and Friends of the Earth, 1990. A citizen's guide to using the law to fight back against the ravages of mining.

Stripmining: Energy, Environment, and Economics. A 50-minute 16mm film on most facets of the issue. Excellent supplement for this section. Available from MCC, Akron, PA 15701.

Steele, Gary. *But When Will It Be Reclaimed?* Livingston, Ky.: ASPI, 1986. An interesting study document that details the impact of the 1977 federal government mine reclamation law on three counties of Kentucky.

U.S. Bureau of Mines Information Circular 8862. "Land Utilization and Reclamation in the Mining Industry 1930-1980." Available from the U.S. Department of Interior Bureau of Mines. A thorough, fact-filled, 50-year study.

U.S. Department of Agriculture. Misc. Publication no. 1082. "Restoring Surface-Mined Land." Basic facts about land reclamation.

Acid Rain

The earth will be completely laid waste
  and totally plundered. . . .
The earth dries up and withers,
  the world languishes and withers,
  the exalted of the earth languish.
The earth is defiled by its people.
      —Isaiah 24:3-5

Acidification (acid rain) ranks among the most serious threats to
the environment in the northern hemisphere. Heavily industrial-
ized areas pump some 90 million tons of sulfur dioxide into the air
each year. Hardest hit are southern Sweden, Norway, parts of
central Europe, and eastern United States.
      —Gaia: An Atlas of Planet Management

15. Acid Rain: Global Threat of Acid Pollution

I think that I shall never see
a smokestack lovely as a tree.
—from a poster, source unknown

The problem of living on borrowed energy has been around for some time. We are burning fossil fuels: coal, oil, and natural gas. One of the adverse consequences of this practice is acid rain, a phenomenon widely recognized for the last two decades.

Acid rain is the term most often used for numerous air pollutants dissolved in precipitation. Most scientists suggest that the term is too narrow to describe the phenomenon of air pollution and its effects on the earth today. Acid deposition better describes the broader process involving interactions between many atmospheric pollutants and the earth.

About 100 million tons of manufactured sulfur dioxide (SO_2) and nitrogen oxides (NO_x) are emitted annually, mainly by coal- or oil-fired power stations and metal smelters. Vehicle exhaust accounts for much of the NO_x emitted.

In the atmosphere, SO_2 and NO_x undergo complex chemical changes that transform them into gaseous or liquid sulfuric acid and nitric acid. The pollutants are deposited further away as acid rain, snow, mist, or fog. NO_x and unburned hydrocarbons in vehicle exhaust gases can react in sunlight to form ozone (see chapter 16). Ozone is now recognized as a major factor in forming acid pollution in the air and in precipitation. Man-made ozone in the lower atmosphere damages crops and plants and may hurt human health and property.

It is estimated that 165,000 tons of sulfur and nitrogen are emitted each day in North America. This is equivalent to 4,200 railway boxcars fully loaded every 24 hours.

Eastern North America receives the most acid rain because of the concentration of industry and people there. Some eastern areas are extremely vulnerable because they lack limestone bedrock, which can act as a buffer to acid rain.

Electric utilities in the U.S., most of which burn high-sulfur coal, produce 70 percent of the SO_2 deposits. The U.S. is responsible for about 50 percent of SO_2 deposition in Canada. Canada is responsible for about 10 percent of SO_2 deposition in the northeastern U.S. A binational pollution control agreement between Canada and the U.S. is essential to control acid rain. Negotiations begun in 1981 have not progressed far, and the political fallout from the acid rain dispute is nearly as bitter as the rain itself.

Death by Acid Rain

Silently, slowly, acid rain is delivering a death blow to life in thousands of lakes and streams across Europe and North America. The rain kills fish, frogs, young plants, forests, crops; damages buildings and roads; corrodes metals and automobile finishes; and threatens public water supplies. All the fish are gone from 100 lakes in the Adirondack Mountains (New York). Nine thousand lakes and 60,000 miles of streams may be vulnerable in the U.S., according to a congressional study. Because of acid precipitation, 140 of Ontario's lakes have been declared biologically dead. The Canadian Ministry of Environment warns that if acid loadings remain constant or increase in the next 10 to 20 years, Ontario could lose much of the aquatic life in 48,000 susceptible lakes.

Within the last three years there has been mounting evidence of damage to forests across much of Europe and North America. In the Erzgebirge Mountains of Czechoslovakia, 247,000 acres of forest are already dead from acid rain. Attempts to reforest the area have failed. West Germany estimates that about 35 percent of the nation's forests (1.2 million acres) are dying from the inside out. The Germans call it *Waldesterben*. They are extremely concerned, and acid rain is the chief suspect.

We have frequently traveled the western end of the Pennsylvania Turnpike. One cannot help but see the rows of dying trees along the turnpike at higher elevations. The dead trees are usually on the side of the road receiving exhaust because of prevailing westerly winds and are high enough to be in concentrated acid (ozone) clouds or fog much of the time.

Our hypothesis is that ozone formed from NO_x and unburned hydrocarbons from the constant truck traffic (cars have better pollution controls) is a major cause of the tree damage.

We know that throughout the Allegheny Mountains the gypsy moth has weakened and killed many trees recently, but these dead trees are not in such neat rows as those killed by exhaust. A call to the Turnpike Commission about the problem brought a response of total unawareness of anything unusual about trees along the turnpike. Pennsylvania State University forestry specialists are researching the impact of acid deposition on trees.

In the few years since it was first recognized, acid rain has become one of the most pressing environmental problems of the century. The U.S. National Academy of Sciences (NAS) estimates that acid rain pollution causes $5 billion or more damage annually in eastern U.S. alone. Man-made air pollution causes the harm, and reducing the pollution would lessen the damage. But the U.S. has failed to endorse an adequate control plan. Why? Largely because the options are not economically or politically attractive.

At binational consultations on acid-rain in January 1984 in New Hampshire and Ontario, the U.S. administration refused to send representatives to explain acid rain cleanup proposals. Recommendations by scientific study panels have been neglected. In March 1981, the National Commission on Air Quality stated, "Congress should require a significant reduction by 1990 in the current level of SO_2 emissions in the eastern United States."

The NAS has made two landmark reports on acid rain. In September 1981 it stated: "It is the Committee's opinion, based on evidence we have examined, that the picture is disturbing enough to merit prompt tightening of restrictions on atmospheric emissions from fossil fuels and other large sources such as metal smelters and cement manufacture.

"Of the options presently available, only the control of emissions of sulfur and nitrogen oxides can significantly reduce the rate of deterioration of sensitive freshwater ecosystems. In the most seriously affected [geographic] areas [average precipitation of pH being 4.0 to 4.5], this would mean a reduction of 50 percent in deposited hydrogen ions."

Then in June 1983 the NAS said, "If we assume that all other factors, including meteorology, remain unchanged, the annual average concentration of sulfur in precipitation at a given site should be reduced in proportion to a reduction in SO_2 and sulfate transported to that site from a source or region of sources."

Earthkeepers' Response

The NAS study concluded that the amount of SO_2 entering the air must be reduced. There are many ways to do this, all with some unattractive characteristics. They include:

- Burn sulfur-free coal.
- Remove the sulfur from coal before burning it.
- Add scrubbers in coal-generating smokestacks to remove sulfur.
- Add lime to burning coal (furnace limestone injection).
- Use petroleum, natural gas, or organic waste biomass instead of coal.
- Use more nuclear power. (Note: it takes 3 percent of U.S. electricity to refine the nuclear fuel used by U.S. nuclear generators today.)
- Use more-efficient electric appliances.
- Use alternate types of energy: solar, hydroelectric, or wind.
- Use less electricity; practice increased conservation.

It is apparent that the issue of acid rain is complex. Christians must consider it in the context of earth stewardship, lifestyle, and justice. How much are we willing to pay in time, convenience, and money to correct this injustice? How concerned are we in caring for God's creation? What about the impact on poor Appalachian areas where high-sulfur coal mining is the basis of the economy?

We can reduce future acid rain deposits. We need the willpower to do what is right in a way that does justice to land and to the people involved.

Discussion Questions

1. Why is acid deposition a more inclusive description of this pollution phenomenon than acid rain?

2. How does acid rain happen? What are the major causes?

3. Discuss the extent of this environmental problem.

4. Review the named reports by the National Academy of Sciences. What are their conclusions?

5. What do you think should be done about acid rain? What can you do to reduce acid rain?

6. Some say not enough is known about acid rain to warrant action. If you agree, what further research or proof is needed?

7. Ask your state, provincial, or federal legislator about the status of acid rain legislation.

Resources

Acid Rain Foundation, Inc., The, 1630 Blackhawk Hills, St. Paul, MN 55722, will supply a catalog and information about recent materials on acid rain.

Acid Rain: Requiem or Recovery. A 27-minute 16mm film by the National Film Board of Canada, 1982. Presents the issue fairly and effectively. Available from MCC, Akron, PA 17501.

McCormick, John. *Acid Earth—The Global Threat of Acid Pollution.* Published by the International Institute for Environment and Development, 1985. From Earthscan, 1717 Massachusetts Ave., N.W., Suite 302, Washington, DC. Best global study available.

Postle, Sandra. *Air Pollution, Acid Rain, and the Future of Forests.* Worldwatch Paper 58. Worldwatch Institute, 1776 Mass. Ave. NW, Washington, DC 20036.

Pringle, Laurence. *Rain of Troubles: The Science and Politics of Acid Rain.* New York: The Macmillan Co., 1988. Brief, readable book.

The Greenhouse Effect

You made [humankind] ruler over the works of your hands;
  you put everything under his feet:
all flocks and herds,
  and the beasts of the field,
the birds of the air,
  and the fish of the sea,
  all that swim the paths of the seas.
O Lord, our Lord,
  how majestic is your name in all the earth!
    —Psalm 8:6-9

The phenomenon of increasing carbon dioxide amounts to a global experiment that we are imposing on our climate, with unprecedented capacity to disrupt our lives and those of future generations. Unfortunately there are no easy solutions.
    —Gaia: An Atlas of Planet Management

16. North American Heat Wave: Greenhouse Effect?

The winter of 1985-86 was mild with an early spring. The summer of 1986 was hot and the next winter, mild and dry. Then came the heat of the summers of 1987 and 1988. Is this part of the global warming trend that climatologists have been predicting? If so, why is it occurring?

There is substantial evidence that the current global warming is due to the so-called greenhouse effect. A number of gases in the earth's atmosphere are called greenhouse gases. They allow incoming solar radiation to pass through readily, but stop some of the heat radiating out from the earth's surface, in the same way heat is trapped by the glass of a greenhouse.

The chief greenhouse gas is carbon dioxide (CO_2). Its concentration in the atmosphere regulates earth's temperature. Recent scientific studies have determined that there are other greenhouse gases important in climate regulation. These include ozone, nitrous oxide, methane, and chlorofluorocarbons (CFCs) that are used as refrigerants, plastic foam blowing agents, and solvents. They eventually find their way into the atmosphere.

There is much recent information on the global warming trend. Worldwatch Institute's annual analysis, *State of the World 1987*, refers to the greenhouse effect extensively. World Resources Institute's annual analyses, *World Resources 1986* and *World Resources*

1987, both have up-to-date and reliable information on the topic. Much of the data for this chapter comes from these sources.

How Bad Is It?

Is global warming actually occurring? Most scientists agree that it is. *State of the World 1987* says: "In late July 1986, a team of scientists studying the effect of rising atmospheric levels of CO_2 and other greenhouse gases, published evidence that the predicted global warming has begun. Meteorologists at the University of East Anglia in the United Kingdom, constructed a comprehensive global temperature series for the last 134 years. Their conclusion: The data show a long time scale warming trend, with the three warmest years being 1980, 1981, and 1983 and five of the nine warmest years in the entire 134 year record occurring after 1978" (p. 3).

World Resources 1987 concurs: "Nineteen eighty-six may well be remembered in science circles as the year when a consensus, of sorts, was reached on global climate change. New, more sophisticated computer models using better data indicate that the earth's climate is growing warmer. And it is doing so faster than scientists had previously predicted. As a result of increasing levels of CO_2 combined with other important trace gases like CFCs, methane, and nitrous oxide, global temperatures may increase 3.5 to 4.2 degrees Celsius by the middle of the next century" (p. 158).

In October 1986, a U.S. geologic survey team reported that the frozen earth beneath the Arctic tundra in Alaska had warmed 4 to 7 degrees Fahrenheit over the last century, further evidence that a CO_2-induced warming trend was under way.

Why are atmospheric levels of CO_2 increasing today? Prior to the modern industrial age, these levels were quite stable. The CO_2 used by green plants to make food was recycled to the air by natural plant and animal respiration and decomposition. In the absence of any major change in the amount of vegetation on the earth, atmospheric levels of CO_2 remained constant.

The increase of CO_2 in earth's air today is the result of two human-related activities: the widespread burning of fossil fuels like coal and petroleum and worldwide destruction of forests and other vegetation.

The *Global 2000 Report* concludes that "18-20 million hectares [50 million acres] of forest is being destroyed annually. This is an area half the size of California." In addition, the report says an area of cropland and grassland the size of the state of Maine is becoming barren wasteland each year.

Greenhouse Gases

As forests and vegetation are destroyed, the CO_2 normally used in their growth remains in the air. The carbon in the trees and plants being destroyed is returned to the air as CO_2 during decomposition. Thus the increase of this greenhouse gas, CO_2.

Scientists estimate that between 1860 and 1980, forest clearing released more than 100 billion tons of carbon into the air. Today, land conversion—chiefly deforestation in the tropics—is estimated to cause a net release of between 0.6 billion and 2.6 billion tons of carbon annually. This is between 12 and 50 percent of the amount released each year by fossil fuel combustion.

As fossil fuels are burned, carbon, stored in the earth for millions of years, is released to the atmosphere in the form of CO_2. According to data in *State of the World 1987*, "Since 1860 the combustion of fossil fuels has released some 185 billion tons of carbon to the atmosphere. Annual emissions rose from an estimated 93 million tons in 1860 to about 5 billion tons at present, a 53-fold increase. The bulk of these emissions occurred since 1950 as the rapid rise in oil use added substantially to carbon releases [already arising] from coal" (p. 158).

In 1860, the CO_2 level in the atmosphere was about 260 parts per million (ppm). Today it is 346 ppm, a 30-percent increase. Just since 1958, when scientists began routinely monitoring CO_2, the concentration of CO_2 has risen 9 percent.

Balancing the carbon equation is not the only step needed to slow global warming. Methane, nitrous oxide, synthetic chlorofluoro carbons, and other trace gases collectively may contribute as much to the apparent greenhouse warming as CO_2.

Most methane is produced by microbes during the breakdown of organic carbon compounds. It apparently remained constant in the earth's atmosphere for many years. Methane began increasing in about 1600. It has more than doubled since then and is now increasing by 1 to 2 percent per year. The exact cause has not been determined, but it is likely due to such human activities as biomass burning, concentration of cattle and hog feeder operations, and widespread rice cultivation. Like CO_2, methane acts as a greenhouse gas trapping heat from the earth. According to *State of the World 1987*, estimates are that methane buildup in the atmosphere by the year 2030 could add 20 to 40 percent to the global warming expected from CO_2.

Scientists believe nitrous oxide is increasing in the air due to overfertilization of soil, concentrated animal wastes such as from livestock feed lots, and, to a lesser degree, fossil fuel burning. Nitrous oxide has recently been found to be a greenhouse gas. Its projected concentration by the year 2030 is expected to increase the global warming trend between 10 and 20 percent over the level expected from CO_2 at that time.

Chlorofluorocarbons (CFCs) are highly stable chemical compounds. The consensus is that continuing emissions of CFCs at current levels would reduce the total amount of ozone by 3 to 5 percent in about 100 years. Ozone (O_3), a variant of oxygen, is present in tiny amounts in the atmosphere. Upper stratospheric ozone shields the earth's surface against ultraviolet radiation. Ozone also occurs in the low stratosphere, where it absorbs heat radiated from the earth. Changes in its concentration affect surface temperatures due to the greenhouse effect. Thus an increase in CFCs and a decrease in ozone will also cause a global warming trend.

Several of the CFC gases are known to be increasing at about 6 percent per year. *World Resources 1986* comments that "production of these gases has been increasing steadily and if it continues to do so, CFCs contribution to the greenhouse effect will be the second largest [after CO_2] during the first half of the next century" (p. 175).

Effects of the Warming Trend

Scientists are approaching consensus that the earth is slowly warming. The next step is to ponder the consequences and decide whether anything can be done about the problem.

In October 1985 a conference was held at Villach, Austria, on greenhouse gases, climate change, and associated impacts. Recommendations from that conference attempt to address those questions.

- Many important economic and social decisions are being made today concerning irrigation, hydropower, and agricultural land use. It is assumed that past climatic data are a reliable guide for the future. This is no longer valid reasoning.

- Climate change and sea level rises due to greenhouse gases are closely linked with other major environmental issues. Some of these are acid deposition and threats to the earth's ozone shield, mostly due to changes in the composition of the atmosphere by human activity.

- Some warming of climate now appears inevitable due to past actions. Yet the rate and degree of future warming could be profoundly affected by governmental policies on energy conservation, use of fossil fuels, and the emission of some greenhouse gases.

- Based on evidence of past climatic changes, climate models project a doubling of the atmospheric CO_2 concentration. There is little doubt that such a great change would have profound effects on global ecosystems, agriculture, water resources, and sea ice.

The conference called on governments to take into account the results of these scientific studies in their policies on social and economic development, environmental programs, and control of emissions of greenhouse gases. Areas of the earth likely to be affected most include the Amazon Basin, the Indian subcontinent, Europe, the Arctic, and the North American Great Lakes region.

Earthkeepers' Response

Long-term atmospheric change is scientifically complex. The fossil fuel producers have their economic interests. Mandating lifestyle changes has a political impact. Therefore, public policy responses to evidence of the greenhouse effect have been slow to emerge. In testimony to Congress in early 1989, two leading scientists gave conflicting testimony. Both agreed that global climatic change could have immense effects, but they disagreed over whether there was enough scientific understanding to justify sweeping environmental legislation, the Associated Press reported (21 February 1989).

Christians concerned about good earth stewardship can do something about the greenhouse effect. First, we must understand and accept that this is a problem Christian earthkeepers should address. We should learn about it. It is a problem caused by humans, and humans can do something about it. An Advisory Group on Greenhouse Gases was established in 1986 as a result of the Villach Conference. It agreed that "limiting emission of the greenhouse gases carbon dioxide, methane, CFCs, ozone and nitrous oxide among others, should be achieved through energy conservation."

Everyone can be involved with energy conservation. We can develop lifestyles that will help reduce greenhouse gas increases. It is ironic that to "beat the heat" people buy and turn up air conditioners that use more electricity, which burns more coal or oil (unless it comes from nuclear power, causing other problems). That releases more CO_2 to the air, which increases the greenhouse effect and contributes to more heat.

We can participate in environmental organizations that keep us informed. We can encourage legislators to pass appropriate regulations. We can use more renewable energy, drive smaller cars, go 55 miles per hour instead of 70, recycle as much as possible.

We can help reforest the earth. We can assist in the restoration and revegetation of wasted and barren lands. This helps to use up excess CO_2.

We must learn to live within the limitations of God's created order, conserving, using renewable resources, and recycling natural resources.

It is only through this kind of living that we will show proper reverence for the Creator, obedience to an appropriate creation theology, and assurance that God's good creation will be maintained for his glory.

17. Ozone Depletion: Environmental Shock

One of the most recent and shocking examples of environmental degradation caused by humans is the depletion of the protective ozone layer in the earth's stratosphere. This ozone layer which shields the earth from the sun's deadly ultraviolet radiation is being destroyed by man-made chemical pollution. Some scientists predict large increases in the number of human skin cancers, cataracts, and immunological dysfunctions; damage to crops and other vegetation; an endangered ocean food web; and possible climatic disturbances as consequences of this destruction.

There is consensus among scientists now that ozone depletion is caused by CFCs. Released at the earth's surface, CFCs ascend to the ozone region 10 to 15 miles up and break into components that include chlorine molecules. One chlorine molecule can destroy thousands of ozone molecules over time. The CFCs are also a greenhouse gas and help retain heat on the surface of the earth.

CFCs were developed in the 1930s and soon were in great demand because of their many desirable characteristics; they were odorless, nonflammable, noncorrosive, nontoxic. They were used in foam insulation and throwaway aerosol propellants. And they were relatively cheap. The depletion of the earth's ozone layer was never imagined as a side effect.

In 1974 two chemists at the University of California discovered that CFCs could destroy ozone. They raised questions about their commercial use, but they were not taken seriously.

Then in 1977 a team of British scientists measuring stratospheric ozone in the Antarctic discovered the ozone layer missing. Their study was continued until 1985. By that time they concluded that there was indeed a large hole in the ozone layer over Antarctica. After much debate, the scientific community concurred with the British scientists that there was a hole in the ozone layer and that CFCs were the cause.

According to *Newsweek* (11 June 1988), 200 researchers from nine countries met in Colorado in May 1988 and concluded that

CFCs are causing the ozone gap. "It is totally unequivocal and straightforward," says atmospheric chemist James Anderson of Harvard. "There would be no ozone hole without fluorocarbons."

Earthkeepers' Response

Even before this meeting there was sufficient consensus on CFCs that 31 countries meeting in Montreal, Quebec, Canada, signed a treaty designed to reduce CFC emissions by 35 to 50 percent by the year 2000. According to the treaty, CFC emissions are to be frozen at current levels in 1989 with actual reductions beginning in 1994. The most recent scientific evidence suggests that this treaty may be too little, too late. On 15 March 1988, just one day after the U.S. Senate ratified the CFC treaty, an international panel of 100 scientists reported that global ozone was disappearing at two to three times the rate previously predicted.

Environmental groups now believe that an 85-percent reduction in CFC emissions will be necessary to stabilize current levels of ozone destruction. The two most widely used forms of CFCs stay in the atmosphere 75 to 100 years. Hence, even if these chemicals were banned tomorrow, it would take the earth 100 years to replenish the ozone already lost.

Discussion Questions

1. Explain why the phenomenon of carbon dioxide buildup in the atmosphere is called the greenhouse effect.

2. What is causing the increase of carbon dioxide and other greenhouse gases in the atmosphere?

3. Weigh evidence for a gradual warming trend on the earth.

4. Discuss and describe the potential consequences of the greenhouse effect.

5. What are the possible adverse consequences of a depleted ozone layer?

6. Ozone is a form of oxygen (isotope O_3) that is an undesirable air pollutant from truck exhausts. Yet it is an essential substance in the upper atmosphere where it protects against radiation. Comment on this apparent paradox.

7. Suggest some specific ways that you can work at the ozone depletion problem.

Resources

Gaia: An Atlas of Planet Management. New York: Anchor-
 Doubleday, 1984. Pages 116-118.

Lyman, Francesca, and others. *The Greenhouse Trap*. Boston:
 Beacon Press, 1990. Sponsored by World Resources Institute.

Schneider, Stephen H. *Global Warming*. San Francisco: Sierra Club
 Books, 1989. Readable, by a leading authority.

State of the World 1987. Worldwatch, 1987. Chapter 9. Worldwatch
 Institute, 1776 Mass. Ave. NW, Washington, DC 20036.

State of the World 1988. Worldwatch, 1988. Chap. 10.

World Resources 1986. Chap. 10. World Resources Institute, 1709
 New York Ave. NW, Washington, DC 20006.

World Resources 1987. World Resources, 1987. Chap. 11.

World Resources 1988-89. World Resources, 1988. Chap. 10.

Forests

The trees of the Lord are well watered,
* the cedars of Lebanon that he planted.*
There the birds make their nests;
* the stork has its home in the pine trees.*
          —Psalm 104:16-17

If I knew the world were coming to an end tomorrow,
* I would still go out and plant my three apple trees today.*
          —Martin Luther King, Jr.

The splendor of his forests and fertile fields
* it will completely destroy. . . .*
And the remaining trees of his forests will be so few
* that a child could write them down.*
          —Isaiah 10:18-19

18. Vanishing Rain Forest: Implications for the Church

The destruction of the tropical rain forest is one of the most startling environmental tragedies of our time. Poor people who must use the rain forest for fuel and farming are putting increasing pressure on this fragile ecosystem. People in developed countries such as Canada and the United States buy rain-forest timber and beef raised on forest-turned-pasture, adding to its rampant destruction.

Those who have the resources to remedy the situation seem oblivious to the tragedy. Unless they soon understand the importance of saving this ecological resource, it may be too late. The loss of the earth's tropical rain forests has moral and ethical implications.

It is important that Christians understand the nature of this problem and take action. Tropical rain forests are in serious jeopardy. Our fast-food lifestyle may be a contributing factor.

Industrialized countries have done well recently to reforest some of the northern coniferous and temperate deciduous forests. These forests are being replenished by reforestation, although acid pollution is threatening them in some regions.

How Bad Is It?

Tropical rain forests are located in some 70 countries, but about 80 percent of the world acreage is in Bolivia, Brazil, Colombia, Gabon, Indonesia, Malaysia, Peru, Venezuela, and Zaire.

The global rain forests are rapidly being decimated. Ellen Hosmer reports in the *Multinational Monitor* (June 1987) that the tropical rain forest is being destroyed at the rate of 17 million acres per year. That is 75,000 acres per day or an area about the size of Pennsylvania per year.

Data from *Gaia: An Atlas of Planet Management* are even more alarming. It reports "the loss figure is 30 million acres per year. We are witnessing the *degradation* of at least a further 25 million acres of forest a year, again mainly in the tropics. From 1950-1975 at least 298 million acres of closed moist forest were destroyed, mostly from South and Southeast Asia. By the end of the century another 672 million acres could be eliminated. . . . [By] 2025, we stand to lose another 747 million acres at least" (p. 42).

By 1980 almost 40 percent of the world's tropical rain forest had been destroyed. A map produced by the Rain Forest Action Network shows that by the year 2000, 60 percent of the original rain forest of the Americas will be gone. In Africa 70 percent will be gone; in Asia, 80 percent.

Says Hosmer, "Without an immediate plan of action—something that is still not on the drawing boards—environmentalists fear that in another 30 to 40 years there may not be a single rain forest to save" (*Multinational Monitor*, June 1987).

The annual rate of tropical rain-forest destruction for selected countries (1981 to 1985) is recorded by the World Resources Institute and the International Institute for Environment and Development in *World Resources 1987*. Two countries losing forested area rapidly are Ivory Coast and Madagascar, with a 5.9 percent annual loss rate. At that rate, in 11.9 years they will have no forest remaining. Paraguay is losing rain forest at the rate of 4.6 percent annually (15 years); Nigeria, 4 percent (17.5 years); Costa Rica and Nepal, 3.9 percent (18 years); and Haiti, 3.4 percent (20.5 years). Many countries have lower rates of deforestation, but large areas of forest are already gone. Examples are Brazil, Indonesia, Peru, India, Zaire, Burma, and Venezuela.

Why Rain Forest Is Cut

The causes of rain-forest loss are clear. John Spears and Edward Ayensa describe the reasons concisely in a chapter of the book *The Global Possible*. They list population pressure, grazing, fuel-wood use, commercial logging, failure of forestry to integrate with development in other sectors, and low levels of investment in forestry.

Two hundred million people live in tropical forests. Population is growing rapidly in some of these regions. Poor people follow the timber harvesters into the forest to eke out a subsistence living. But rain-forest soil is usually not adequate to support agricultural crops for long. Conditions there accelerate decomposition and denitrification (loss of nitrogen). The soil quickly becomes infertile, and without rain-forest canopy the exposed soil is soon degraded.

Peasant farmers then go further into the rain forest, slashing and burning more land for farming, and the degradation process continues. In many countries the best land is used by wealthy landowners for cash or export cropping. The poor are forced into the rain forest to farm for survival.

The increasing gathering of fuel wood to meet the needs of expanding populations also puts great pressure on the world's rain forests. According to the *Gaia* atlas, fuel-wood gathering depletes at least five million acres of tropical rain forest each year and at least twice as much open woodland and scrub forest.

Over half the world's five billion inhabitants depend upon firewood for fuel. More than one billion people live in areas where the collection of wood already outpaces new growth. The U.N. Food and Agriculture Organization reports that more than 100 million people—half of them in Africa—cannot get enough fuelwood to meet their basic needs. Nearly 1.2 billion people are meeting their fuel-wood needs by overcutting and depleting their forests. By the year 2000 more than half these people will either lack sufficient fuel-wood or meet their needs by depleting the resource further.

Sandra Postle of Worldwatch Institute states in *Natural History* magazine (April 1985) that "meeting the Third World's projected fuel-wood needs by the year 2000 would require a thirteen-fold increase in the current rate of tree planting for nonindustrial use. Now only one acre of trees is planted for every 10 acres cleared. The gap is greatest by far in Africa, where the ratio of tree clearing to planting is 29 to 1."

In Latin America and some parts of Africa, wealthy cattle ranchers buy up rain-forest land abandoned by peasant slash-and-burn farmers. After a few years this land is not able to provide enough vegetative growth even for the cattle. Much of the beef from cattle raised in these Latin American rain-forest areas is imported by U.S. fast-food chains. Ellen Hosmer, quoted earlier, says that certain of these companies have come under fire for importing such beef. How these chains respond is yet to be seen.

"To knock five cents off a fast-food hamburger, the United States is importing beef when we produce too much," says biologist Paul Ehrlich of Stanford University. "The result is the deforestation of Central America."

Between 1966 and 1978, Brazil lost over 20 million acres of rain forest to cattle ranching, doubling its beef production in the last 20 years. However, as beef production has increased in Central America, beef consumption there has decreased. Not only does beef raising not feed the developing world's hungry, it also takes away resources needed to produce sustainable food alternatives.

Effects of Rain Forest Loss

The importance of the world's rain forests to the well-being of creation cannot be overstated. Rain forests act as sponges to hold moisture. They help regulate the humidity of the earth's climate. Rain-forest vegetation holds fragile tropical soil and retards erosion.

Tropical rain forests help to stabilize the world's climate by absorbing vast amounts of solar radiation. When the forests are destroyed, the land surface radiates more heat back into space. This can lead to a disruption of convection patterns, wind currents, and rainfall over much of the globe. Rain forests remove carbon dioxide (CO_2) from the air, store the carbon, and release oxygen. Thus they counteract the greenhouse effect and serve as lungs for the earth's atmosphere.

Perhaps the most important function of the rain forest is the maintenance of the earth's most biologically diverse ecosystem. Rain forests hold nearly half the world's known plant and animal species. As rain forest is destroyed, so are many of its species. The U.S. National Academy of Science reports that "nearly 1 million species face extinction by the year 2000 because of deforestation."

The *Gaia* atlas states, "If present [deforestation] trends continue, we can expect an annual rate of loss as high as 50,000 species by the year 2000. At that point we would be driving 130 species into extinction every day."

It is sad that human beings, charged with the care of God's created organisms, are so callously allowing them to become extinct. We are not only allowing this to happen, we are actively hastening the process.

The loss of rain-forest species has another dimension. The genetic diversity of the living things there is important in agricultural plant and animal breeding programs. Especially food-crop plants need to have genes from the wild incorporated occasionally to keep them healthy and productive.

Rain forests are important in two other ways. They serve as a repository of naturally occurring drugs that benefit us. For example, from the rain forest come drugs to treat high blood pressure, Hodgkin's disease, multiple sclerosis, Parkinson's disease, and leukemia. A study of the Costa Rican rain forest found that 15 percent of the plants checked there had potential as anticancer agents.

Finally, rain forests are the source of many useful industrial products such as oils, gums, resins, tannin, waxes, alcohols, bamboo, spices, dyes, and timber.

Earthkeepers' Response

How can rain forests be saved? The causes of rain-forest degradation are clear. The reversal of the destruction, though not easy, is possible.

From the significant Global Possible Conference in 1984, a group of concerned scientists derived "five priority goals through which it should be possible to contain deforestation in the most critically affected developing countries by the turn of the century."

Their goals are (1) to rehabilitate 150 million hectares of seriously degraded tropical watersheds; (2) to preserve 100 million hectares of threatened forest ecosystems; (3) to increase fuel-wood planting rates fivefold by the year 2000; (4) to improve and expand industrial forestry; and (5) to strengthen forestry research, education, and training.

A plan for implementing these goals would include actions to:

• Provide farmers in degraded watersheds with the materials, credit, and technical support they need to improve farm productivity, control grazing and logging, and to check runoff and erosion.

• Provide international assistance for ecological surveys to select conservation sites and for purchase and maintenance of conservancy areas.

• Create a new international fund to subsidize the establishment of protected forests through the leadership of the industrial countries which will reap many of the benefits.

• Channel land-settlement projects into unforested lands, introduce land reform, employment programs, and agroforestry.

• Lay the groundwork for large-scale fuel-wood planting in the 1990s by greatly expanding tree nurseries, credit and extension programs, and demonstration woodlots.

• Encourage private-sector participation in tree farming.

• Shift the emphasis in tropical forestry research toward sociological aspects of forestry.

• Introduce training programs to reorient forest services from a policing mission to providing technical extension support to small farmers, cooperatives, and others.

Development agencies such as Mennonite Central Committee (MCC) are well equipped to implement such goals and action plans as those suggested by the Global Possible Conference. MCC already has workers in many countries where the tropical rain forest is being destroyed. MCC works at integrated development. Combining such programs as agriculture, health, education, community development, and reforestation is likely the most appropriate way to work at rain-forest conservation.

In light of the rapidity of rain-forest destruction, those able to respond should do so with a sense of urgency. Individuals can do some of the following to help conserve the rain forest:

• Support MCC development work. MCC workers have done a respectable job in helping the poor and in planting trees, two good ways to help save the rain forest.

• Volunteer for a term of service in a rain-forest country.

• Get training in forestry or environmental science, and make yourself available to MCC.

• Insist that any beef you eat not come from rain-forest pastures. Check out local restaurants, asking managers to discover the source of their beef.

• Use local timber and building materials where possible. Do you really need that mahogany? In 1983 the United States imported over $3 billion more timber than was exported—this in a land of vast coniferous and hardwood forest and only 240 million people.

• Live ecologically. Use only what you need. Share your abundance.

• Pray that people everywhere may become protectors, stewards, and proper caretakers of God's creation, including the magnificent rain forest.

Discussion Questions

1. Evaluate who is most responsible, directly and indirectly, for the destruction of the rain forest.

2. Review the description of the fuel-wood crisis. What is the problem, and what do you think should be done about it?

3. Discuss the ecological importance of the tropical rain forest.

4. What is the hamburger connection with the rain forests? Express your analysis of this activity. What are some solutions?

5. To what extent do you think that earth's species should be preserved? Relate this to Christian responsibility for creation stewardship.

6. Study the Global Possible Conference goals and actions listed. How do you think the rain forest should be preserved?

7. What can you do to help preserve earth's forests? Are you ready to commit yourself to specific actions?

Resources

Firewood, The Other Energy Crisis. A 15-minute 16mm United Nations film. Shows effects of deforestation and soil erosion. Available on free loan from MCC, Akron, PA 17501.

Gaia: An Atlas of Planet Management. New York: Anchor-Doubleday, 1984. See sections on the rain forest.

"Paradise Lost: The Ravaged Rainforest." *Multinational Monitor.* June 1987. This entire issue is on rain forests. Back copies available from *Multinational Monitor*, P.O. Box 19405, Washington, DC 20036. An excellent resource!

Repetto, Robert, ed. *The Global Possible: Resources, Development and the New Century.* New Haven, Conn.: Yale University Press, 1985.

Repetto, Robert, and Malcolm Gillis, eds. *Public Policies and the Issue of Forest Resources.* New York: Cambridge University Press, 1988.

State of the World 1985, 1986, 1987, 1988. Worldwatch Institute, 1776 Mass. Ave. NW, Washington, DC 20036. See parts on rain forests.

Vanishing Earth/Earth Music, The. VHS video cassette. 1985. Shows environmental degradation and forest destruction in the Philippines. Two programs on one cassette (30 minutes, 25 minutes). Available on free loan from MCC, Akron, PA 17501.

World Resources 1986, 1987. World Resources Institute, 1709 New York Ave. NW, Washington, DC 20006. See relevant sections.

Worldwatch Papers: *Food or Fuel: New Competition for the World's Cropland* (Paper 35); and *On the Brink of Extinction: Conserving Biological Diversity* (78). From Worldwatch Institute.

PART THREE

Environment and Conflict

Environmental Degradation Related to Conflict

Many shepherds will ruin my vineyard
and trample down my field;
they will turn my pleasant field
into a desolate wasteland.
It will be made a wasteland,
parched and desolate before me;
the whole land will be laid waste
because there is no one who cares.
Over all the barren heights in the desert
destroyers will swarm,
for the sword of the Lord will devour
from one end of the land to the other;
no one will be safe.
They will sow wheat but reap thorns;
they will wear themselves out but gain nothing.
So bear the shame of your harvest
because of the Lord's fierce anger.
          —Jeremiah 12:10-13

If Central America were not racked with poverty, there would be no
revolution. If Central America were not racked with hunger, there
would be no revolution. If Central America were not racked with
injustices, there would be no revolution.
          —U.S. Senator Christopher J. Dodd,
             responding to President Reagan's address
             to the Congress on Central America, April 27, 1983

19. Militarism, Development, and World Hunger

Peace cannot be taken in isolation: hunger, oppression, injustice, un-employment, lack of meaning, are all causes of conflict. To work on these causes is therefore to work for peace. . . . The time absolutely must come when the world spends on peace what it now spends on war.
  —Robert Muller, *A Planet of Hope*

The world is rapidly becoming an armed camp. Increasing militarization of society is depressing the quality of human life around the world. The 120 wars since 1945 diverted essential resources from human development programs. The result has been increasing poverty, hunger, and oppression. Refugees dot the globe.

The purpose of this chapter is to raise awareness of the dramatic arms buildup and to identify some of the connections between militarization and development at home and abroad. Education on this issue is critically important if Christians are to respond appropriately to human need.

How Bad Is It?

It is difficult to comprehend the dramatic increases in military spending worldwide in the past decade—almost 20 times pre-

World War II budgets. This twentyfold increase vastly exceeds the increase in world population and the economic base that supports it. Lester R. Brown of the Worldwatch Institute states that "global military expenditures in 1985 of $940 billion exceeded the income of the poorest half of humanity." That poorest half of humanity lives on $300 per capita per year or less.

The U.S. and the U.S.S.R. lead the way in the arms race. Together they comprise just 11 percent of the world's population, but account for over half of the world's military expenditures. The two superpowers each spend around $300 billion annually for "defense." This represents 6.9 percent of the U.S. gross national product (GNP) and 14 percent of the U.S.S.R.'s.

The industrialized countries are the biggest military spenders by far. They represent less than one-fourth of the world's people but spend more than three-fourths of the world's arms budget.

The most rapid growth in military spending recently, however, has been in some parts of the Third World. Purchase of weapons by oil-rich countries has helped boost military spending fivefold in the last 25 years. Per-capita military spending in a recent year illustrates this: Saudi Arabia, $2,579; Qatar, $2,222; Oman, $1,548. The figure for Israel is $1,301. For the U.S. it is $845; for Canada, $252. Some Third-World countries do not spend much on the military—but they do not spend much for development either. Per-capita military expenditures that same year for Somalia were $20; for Ethiopia and Mozambique, $13.

Along with the rapid growth of military spending in the Third World has come military rule. Since 1960, the number of countries ruled by military governments has grown from 22 to 57. Over one billion people (one in five) now live in such countries.

Effects of Militarization

When one compares military expenditures with development expenditures around the world, misdirected priorities are apparent. In a recent year, world military expenditures for each soldier averaged $25,600. Only $450 was spent per child for education; for health research, $11 per capita. During that year the U.S. spent $89,228 per soldier and $686 per school child. Canada spent U.S.

$75,707 for each soldier and U.S. $936 per school child.

Between 450 million and 1.3 billion of the 5 billion people in the world today are hungry. The World Bank refers to 800 million persons as being the "absolute poor." There are over 10 million refugees around the world. Another 4.5 million people are refugees within their own countries, and 3 million refugees have been accepted for resettlement in other countries.

Most of the world's hungry, poor, and refugees are in the Third World. And that is where the wars, revolutions, and conflicts are. It is no coincidence. War and revolution cause hunger, poverty, and refugees. Poor and hungry people cause revolution. The two are intertwined.

Frank Barnaby in a recent article in *South Magazine* says, "The Third World War has begun—in the Third World. Presently there are 50 wars or conflicts in progress. One in four nations is involved. On average a new war begins somewhere in the world every three months. In the 40 years since the Second World War, the territory of about 80 countries and the armed forces of about 90 states have been involved in war."

It is the view of many that the primary factor in the recent African hunger crisis was war. Countries with the most hungry people and the most refugees were involved in conflicts. Examples are Ethiopia, Sudan, Chad, Mozambique, Angola, and Somalia.

The Scandal of the Arms Trade

The industrialized countries, especially the superpowers, provide arms to unstable Third-World countries. This is well documented. Ruth Leger Sivard says in her 1985 study, *World Military and Social Expenditures*: "In the 20 years ending in 1983, eight countries accounted for 85 percent of the $308 billion in world arms trade. The United States and U.S.S.R. alone had two-thirds of the export trade. The largest market for arms was in the developing countries." That preparation-for-war market amounted to $223 billion in that twenty-year period.

Fifty-four countries are now in the business of selling arms in foreign markets, according to Sivard. She notes, "Sales are seen as an aid to balance of payments and for the big arms-producing countries as a means of holding down costs by extending production runs and sharing research expenditures.

"Arms assistance in the form of gifts to poorer countries may also be used to facilitate military-basing arrangements or as an integral part of foreign policy. Since 1946 the U.S. alone has provided gifts of $47 billion to developing countries for military training and equipment."

One result of the arms trade has been the fostering of a dangerous alliance between governments and private arms dealers in the developed countries. Another result is the promotion of the use of sophisticated weapons in unstable countries. The weapons and advisors are provided to the governing elite of developing nations. This allows the elite to control and oppress the majority of the population. Thus are the poor and the hungry "contained."

The developed countries have loaned money (often at high interest rates) to unstable Third-World countries. Much of that money has been used to purchase arms to protect those in power. Arms purchases in many countries have added an incredible foreign debt burden. In Latin America interest payments on the $368 billion debt are consuming 36 percent of the region's export earnings. To counteract the debt burden, countries institute "austerity programs" demanded by creditors, cutting out human services and raising food prices. This causes further instability and more oppressive behavior. The hungry and the poor suffer.

Guns or Butter?

Third-World countries do need appropriate assistance for development from the industrial countries. Unfortunately, the amount of foreign aid has been decreasing in recent years. At present the U.S. is spending about 7 percent of its GNP on defense and only 0.23 percent on development aid. It ranks last of 17 countries in the Organization for Economic Cooperation and Development (OECD) in most recent data. Canada provides 0.49 percent of its GNP for Third-World development assistance and ranks eighth in the OECD.

One thing more should be said about U.S. foreign aid. In a recent year the U.S. provided twice as much money for "security" aid or arms to developing countries as it did for development aid for people programs. Of $14 billion, $9.2 billion was for "security" aid.

Militarism also flourished in the U.S. Budget authority for U.S. national defense has doubled since the Reagan administration took office, rising from $143.9 billion in fiscal year (FY) 1980, to $286.1 billion in FY 1986, a real growth rate of 46.75 percent after inflation. The administration's request for $320.3 billion for FY 1987 (a real growth rate of 8.2 percent) was reduced a bit by Congress to $292 billion.

While military spending is still increasing, programs for the poor are still being cut. The administration had requested budget cuts (or cancellation of programs for the poor) worth $8.2 billion in FY 1987. Fourteen low-income programs were to be terminated completely; 15 would not be funded for the rest of 1986. Again Congress saved some of this funding, but not all. This occurred at a time when over 30 million Americans were living below the poverty level and 10 million were hungry.

The U.S. (as well as the rest of the world) cannot have both "guns and butter." The purchase of guns adds to an incredible national debt of almost $3 trillion, a deficit which people like Mortimer Adler consider one of the two most critical national problems in the U.S. today.

Numerous guns-versus-butter comparisons could be made. Here are several to illustrate:

- F-16 Falcon jet fighter planes cost $18 million each. The Army wanted 216 more of these for 1987. The total cost of these 216 planes was equal to all the low-income programs that were cut in 1987—about $4 billion.

- The price of a single F-16 plane was equivalent to the annual salaries of 900 teachers at $20,000 per year. The cost of one B-1 bomber would pay 25,000 teachers!

- The Pentagon spent as much for annual newspapers and magazine subscriptions as the entire budget for the Peace Corps ($124 million).

Sometimes it is claimed that military spending is good for the economy. It is, for a few people. But data from the U.S. Bureau of Labor Statistics reveal that $1 billion invested in the defense industry creates only about 75,000 jobs. The same amount invested in civil engineering creates 110,000 jobs; in consumer goods production, 112,000 jobs; in health care systems or education, 138,000 jobs.

Canada is also a major spender for defense in the world scene. The Canadian Department of National Defence (DND) will spend $11.5 billion during fiscal year 1988-89. Although the U.S. spends more each year, the Canadian government's spending for defense "has outpaced the massive increases in U.S. defense spending under the Reagan administration. While the U.S. defense budget grew about 44 percent in real terms since 1980, the Canadian defense budget grew about 50 percent in real terms," reports the June 1988 issue of the *Ploughshares Monitor*, a publication of the Ontario-based Project Ploughshares.

Forty-three percent of Canada's federal government discretionary spending goes to national defense. Canada is in the top 10 percent of the military spenders worldwide and is the 12th largest military spender in the world.

Military Spending Retards Development

Duane K. Friesen, in the recent book *Christian Peacemaking and International Conflict*, lists four inhibiting effects of military spending on desired economic development: "It increases inflation, it uses up scarce materials, it absorbs a large portion of the world's scientists and engineers, and it diverts capital from poor countries who need that capital to solve basic social and economic problems."

But what does all this have to do with us? Aren't these mostly government decisions beyond our control? How can we be held responsible for others' decisions?

Mennonite Central Committee (MCC) U.S. Peace Section staff members Linda and Titus Peachey describe the dilemma caused by the recent militarism of the U.S. They say: "Our very distance from the suffering and violence of war is one of the most crucial aspects of militarism today. As citizens of a superpower we live very protected lives while our factories, resources, and research talent create huge arsenals of death and devastation. . . . It is diffi-

cult to identify one's own responsibility. Whereas war preparations once meant war bonds and military conscription, today's
militarism has so permeated our society that it is difficult to pin-
point who is involved and where the responsibility lies."

The Peacheys illustrate our militarized society:

• Over 30,000 North American companies now hold prime
military contracts with the U.S. government. An estimated
150,000 companies do subcontract work for the prime contractors. About 15 million contracts are signed yearly.

• The United States allocates 70 percent of federally funded
research and development monies to military-related efforts.

• Over 50 percent of federal tax dollars go to the military.

• Many of the top 35 companies that supply the military also
supply our consumer products. General Electric, Westinghouse,
Honeywell, IBM, GM, ITT, Ford, and Singer are some.

The military, industrial, and political interests in our society are
closely linked. Military contractors subcontract throughout the
country. This puts pressure on legislators to vote to fund the military to bring jobs to their areas. Many retired Pentagon officials
take top-ranking jobs with military-related industries. Perceived
threats to U.S. security are quickly translated by politicians into
larger and larger defense budgets. Each superpower wants to bar-
gain from a "position of strength."

Even small communities across North America are discovering
that more and more jobs contribute goods and services to the military and depend on military funding. Mennonites are increasingly involved with subcontractors working for the military. Mennonite scientists and engineers find it more and more difficult to find
jobs not related to the military.

Earthkeepers' Response

How can we respond to this situation? Our first response to the
militarization of society should be one of understanding the issue.
Then there must be a rediscovery of what the Bible and Jesus have
to say about peace, justice, oppression, hunger, and poverty. As
Christians, our role is to evangelize the world and, at the same
time, work for the shalom described by Jesus and the prophets. It

is true that individual hearts must be transformed for peace and justice to be achieved. But when that transformation occurs, there must be some active response to the evils in our surrounding society. Ways must be found to respond.

Duane Friesen suggests three levels of response to the crisis in military spending. "Most basic," he says, "is to try to find an alternative system of security that need not rely so exclusively on military power. At a second level, we need to seek to influence public policy, especially in more developed countries, to devote a greater portion of their GNP to economic aid for the purpose of solving social problems. At a third level, we need to restructure the civilian economy so that it is no longer so dependent upon military appropriation to provide employment and economic well-being. In the long run, the economy would prosper from a conversion from military spending to other kinds of programs such as health and education."

As we choose ways to respond to the militarism that permeates our society we will need to find answers to some complex questions. The Peacheys list some of them:

- Can we say that we do not participate in preparations for war simply because we do not enlist in the military?

- What should we do if the company we work for makes weapons, but also donates money to charity?

- How much should we try to ensure that our banking, investment, and business practices reflect our commitment to peace?

- Are we responsible if our government uses our tax money for making weapons or financing war?

- If we buy a typewriter or a refrigerator from a leading military contractor, are we supporting the production of weapons?

- What is our responsibility toward people in other countries who are hurt by weapons made in our factories or are simply kept poor by our supplying weapons to the local government?

For people interested in specific action on the U.S. military tax issue, Peacheys' leaflet, "Stages of Conscientious Objection to Military Taxes," has pertinent information. It suggests that one starts by understanding that paying taxes for military purposes conflicts with the testimony of historic peace churches. Paying taxes for military purposes directly and personally involves us in militarism. After understanding, people move to stages that require action. They can decide to "say yes" and take positive actions for peace such as:

- Increase your contributions to religious, charitable, and peace organizations.
- Adjust your lifestyle and priorities so that you can live below the taxable level.
- Work for passage of the Peace Tax Fund Act.
- Join or form a support group.
- Join a volunteer program such as VS, MCC, or BVS.
- Be involved in conflict mediation and peacemaking locally.

One can also decide to say "no" and work at opposing payment of taxes for military purposes in these ways:

- Pay federal taxes under protest.
- Pay the tax due but make the check out to the Department of Health and Human Services instead of the IRS.
- Refuse to pay the federal excise telephone tax.
- Refuse to pay a portion of tax due as a symbol of protest.
- Pay only the nonmilitary portion of tax due. Send the rest to a peace organization or other charity. Accept the consequences as part of submitting to government (Romans 13:1).

Militarism is rampant in our world today. The *Christian Science Monitor* published a series of articles in 1986-87 entitled "Agenda for the Twenty-First Century." Practically every world figure interviewed put the arms race and the nuclear issue at the top of a global problems list.

Militarism affects the most important human problems in our world today. It is partly responsible for hunger, poverty, oppression, and environmental degradation. It produces most of the world's refugees.

Practically every relief, development, and justice issue with which MCC is involved is intertwined with the militarization of society at home and abroad. To remain a credible relief and development agency resourcing people "In the name of Christ," MCC continues to address the problem of militarism. New ways of responding to this major issue will need to be found if we are to be faithful to the call of Christ to be peacemakers in a broken world.

20. War, Conflict, and Environmental Degradation

Too little attention has been paid by Christians to the negative effects of modern warfare and the worldwide arms buildup on the natural environment. Even less attention has been paid to the phenomenon of environmental degradation as a source of war and conflict.

War directly effects the environment, and the arms buildup has an indirect effect on the environment. There is evidence that war and revolution are the result of environmental degradation. We need to consider Christian responses.

Without a healthy natural world, there can be no peace among people and nations. To work at achieving a healthy environment is to work at significant peacemaking in today's world. The church is called to give these activities much higher priority.

War Destroys the Earth

Roger Shinn, professor of social ethics at New York's Union Theological Seminary, says that "war, along with everything else that is said about it, remains the most ecologically destructive of all human activities."

Conventional warfare has always harmed the environment. Modern weapons, including nuclear, chemical, and biological devices, are so environmentally destructive that the only rational hope is that they will never be used.

Atomic bombs dropped by the U.S. on Hiroshima and Nagasaki have demonstrated their awful destructiveness and their tragic consequences to people and the environment. Today's arsenal of weapons has such potential destructiveness as to be almost unimaginable.

Ruth Sivard, in *World Military and Social Expenditures 1985*, says that "the nuclear connection has magnified the danger of war fought even with conventional weapons far beyond anything previously known to civilization." It is sobering to ponder Sivard's "map of the nuclear world, 1985," in the same edition. This map shows 67 countries and territories around the world, identifying locations that harbor over 50,000 nuclear weapons: 170 air bases, 48 naval bases, 90 missile bases, 128 sites for weapon research and production, 104 command centers, and 57 test sites. Also appearing are 516 nuclear power reactors and 375 nuclear research reactors. "These," Sivard says, "were once promoted as 'Atoms for Peace' but now they also carry dangers of mass destruction in the event of war and in the course of regular operations through malfunction, sabotage or the diversion of their by-product to military uses."

The direct effects of chemical warfare have been well illustrated by the foliar destruction in the Vietnam War. The damage done to Vietnam's environment is one of the most extreme cases of ecological destruction by war ever witnessed on earth. Between one-fourth and one-half of the land of Vietnam suffered defoliation at some point during the war. According to a report issued by the International Union for the Conservation of Nature, "much of the damage in Vietnam can probably never be repaired." U.S. herbicide teams dumped about six pounds of chemicals for every South Vietnamese citizen, destroying vegetation and poisoning the land with dioxin. The war also damaged as much as 41 percent of the mangrove forests there.

There is concern that the kind of military-initiated environmental destruction that took place in Vietnam could be repeated in Central America. These comments appear in the article "Militarization: The Environmental Impact" (Green Paper no. 3 of the Environmental Project on Central America):

> For years the region has suffered ecological degradation brought on by deforestation, soil erosion, pesticides pollution and industrial contamination. Now C.A.'s environment faces a more immediate threat. . . . From Panama to Guatemala the armies of the region are stockpiling weaponry that could erase in hours the natural beauty that has taken millennia to evolve. The bombs, bulldozers and defoliants that played so central a role in the Vietnam War are resurfacing on this side of the world, threatening to destroy human life and natural ecosystems.

Preparation for War Squanders Resources

Modern warfare wreaks havoc on today's fragile ecosystems. But preparation for war also has detrimental effects upon the environment and natural resources. Escalating military expenditures divert much-needed human and financial resources from essential economic and environmental development. Some careless defense industries pollute the environment while the military uses scarce natural resources.

The United Nations claims that nearly $1 trillion is now spent annually on military armaments worldwide. That figure exceeds the total income of the poorest half of the earth's people. The stated purpose of military expenditures is "to provide security." The evidence is that military spending is actually doing the opposite. Casebolt and Rauh in an article in the *Sierra Club Yodeler* (June 1986) write:

> In our age of super weaponry, tensions are being aggravated by the appalling contrast between military spending and spending to care for basic human needs and restoration of the environment. We are creating at one and the same time the super weaponry of technological sophistication and power and the conditions—human poverty and inequity and anxiety over an exhausted natural environment—that will lead to war which the weapons of mass destruction are supposed to prevent.

The escalation of the arms race goes hand in hand with a global increase in poverty, hunger, and environmental degradation. This statement stands in a "draft for the final document" of a U.N. Conference *On the Relationship Between Disarmament and Development* held in 1987:

> The continuing arms race is absorbing far too great a proportion of the world's human, financial, natural and technological resources, placing a heavy burden on the economies of all countries. . . . Coming close to the staggering figure of $1 trillion a year, the global military expenditure is in dramatic contrast to economic and social under-development, to the misery and poverty afflicting more than two-thirds of mankind and to the continuing crisis of the world economic system.

Further on, the statement describes the incredible increase in military spending:

> The current level of global military spending incurred worldwide in pursuit of real and perceived security interest, represents a real increase of between four and five times since the end of the Second World War. It also reflects 6 percent of world output and is over 25 times as large as all official development assistance to developing countries.

The world is now spending a lot of money on so-called security which it should be spending on environmental conservation, research, and enhancement. The U.N. statement goes on:

> Diversion of resources for military purposes always amounts to a commensurate reduction of resources for the civilian sector. . . . It is estimated that U.S. $14 trillion at 1983 prices have been spent for military purposes since 1960 worldwide. During this period the increase in world output was $8.6 trillion. Thus, since 1960, military expenditure has absorbed all the economic growth and more.

Lester R. Brown in *State of the World 1986* also notes the waste of human resources for militarization of the world:

> Each year the world spends several times as much on research to increase destructiveness of weapons as on attempts to raise the productivity of agriculture. Indeed, expenditures on weapons research in which half a million scientists are now employed exceed the combined spending on developing new energy technologies, improving human health, raising agricultural productivity and controlling pollution.

The U.S. has in recent years even increased military spending at the expense of the environment. Casebolt and Rauh cited earlier refer to a 1984 report in the *Bulletin of the Atomic Scientist* that overall federal spending increased by 41 percent since 1981. During the same period military spending increased by 70 percent, but spending for conservation and pollution control programs decreased 44 and 19 percent respectively.

Meanwhile, environmental problems cry out for resolution.

Human population has reached 5 billion in a world of dwindling supplies of topsoil, rain forests, pure groundwater, and pure air.

The Military Pollutes the Environment

The military establishment is seen by some observers as the major industrial polluter of the environment today. A chapter on "Military Contamination" in the 1985 book *Troubled Water* by Jonathan King documents this in a convincing way. He notes:

• By its own estimates, the U.S. Department of Defense (DOD) generates 1 billion pounds of hazardous material each year, dwarfing the amount produced by most private companies. The Navy alone says that its ship-and-shore activities in the U.S. generate 19 million gallons of liquid hazardous waste and 35 million pounds of hazardous waste solids each year.

• The military-industrial complex employs over 4 million persons. It produces numerous toxic wastes from paints, solvents, heavy metals, production of explosives and chemical warfare agents, pesticides, and PCBs.

• The U.S. Department of Energy's (DOE) main job is developing and manufacturing nuclear weapons. The DOE maintains 10 nuclear weapon facilities with a combined land area greater than the state of Delaware. The DOE produces large amounts of chemical wastes, much of it contaminated with radioactivity.

King describes how the military uses primitive ways of disposing toxic wastes. DOD has more than 400 facilities handling and storing waste. He describes how one of these sites (discovered by the EPA) in southern California threatens the drinking water supply for 500,000 people. The 27-square-mile Rocky Mountain Arsenal near Denver, Colorado, is described as being "laced with contaminated land and water." King cites numerous other "discoveries" around the U.S. that severely indict the military establishment for its toxic pollution.

Like the Pentagon, the DOE conducts its own environmental monitoring. The EPA is essentially powerless to investigate military pollution, let alone control it. The Ohio attorney general spearheaded an effort in 1988 to hold the federal government accountable for radioactive contamination at decades-old DOE sites.

By late 1988, the DOE had accepted responsibility and made an initial study of a cleanup procedure at the Fernald site near Cincinnati. In February 1989, it admitted its original cost estimate of $68 billion was too low because the first round of estimates of the environmental damage had been too conservative.

The Arms Race Threatens Creation

The resource base upon which human society and all life exists —God's good creation—is clearly in jeopardy. The time has come to recognize that the earth cannot afford both guns and butter. Environmental preservation and restoration and the present arms race are not compatible. The U.N.'s Environment Report says it well: "It can be stated without hesitation [that] the question of disarmament, development and environmental protection are closely linked. . . . A healthy environment cannot be guaranteed amid a widening and escalating arms race."

It is indeed time for all Christians to join the many scientists and politicians who are deploring the arms race. War itself is an intolerable threat to the created world. In addition, the preparation for war is diverting needed resources from environmental salvation and is actually contributing to a poisoned environment.

The Washington, D.C.-based Peace and Environment Project in an "initial draft summary on world peace and common security" has developed a "platform for a healthy, just, and sustainable environment." The opening paragraph relates to this discussion:

> In view of our steadily deteriorating environment, particularly in the industrial nations, we suggest that the U.S. offer to cooperate with the U.S.S.R. and other nations in a Global Environmental Recovery Race. . . . The vast amount of money and scientific know-how that is now wasted on a sterile arms race could be dedicated to meeting the challenges presented by carbon dioxide build-up in the atmosphere, ozone depletion, acid rain, toxic waste and pollution, deforestation and loss of tropical rain forests, groundwater depletion and pollution, soil conservation, species preservation, renewable energy, renewal of ocean and freshwater life and solving worldwide food, hunger, and carrying capacity crises.

The relationship between environmental degradation and conflict is being increasingly studied by those working at peacemaking. In late 1986, a three-day workshop took place in Oslo, Norway, on the theme "the environmental dimension to security issues." Convened by the Norwegian Minister of Defense, participants attended from many European research and peace study institutions.

Norman Myers, world-respected environmental consultant from Oxford, England, wrote about the meeting in the *Bulletin of the Atomic Scientist* (June 1987). The workshop called theorists to "move beyond traditional thinking about security concepts and begin considering a series of environmental factors underpinning the material welfare."

The identified factors include such natural resources as soil, water, forests, grasslands, and fisheries. These prime components of a nation's natural resource essentially maintain the life-support systems of any nation.

If a country's environmental foundations are disturbed or depleted, its economy may well decline, its social fabric deteriorate, and its political structure may become destabilized. The likely outcome is conflict, whether in the form of disorder or revolution within the nation or war with other nations.

Myers' summary: "National security, therefore, is no longer about fighting forces and weaponry alone. It relates increasingly to watersheds, croplands, forests, genetic resources, climate, and other factors rarely considered by military experts and political leaders."

Conflict or Conservation?

Peter Thacher, former deputy executive director of the United Nations Environment Program, gave a speech on worldwide deforestation. He phrased the issue bluntly: "The ultimate choice is between conservation or conflict. Trees now or tanks later. The choice for governments is either to find the means by which to pay now to stop the destruction of the natural resource base, or be prepared to pay later, possibly in blood."

Ulf Svensson of the Swedish Foreign Ministry wrote on this in the preface to John Galtung's book, *Environment, Development and Military Activity*: "Just as wars lead to further degradation of the environment, an environment less able to sustain human societies as we know them today may easily lead to even more wars, in a struggle for even scarcer resources, such as uncontaminated soil and water. This is a vicious circle we cannot afford to be dragged into."

In the final report of the U.N. Group of Governmental Experts on the Relationship between Disarmament and Development is this statement: "There can no longer be the slightest doubt that resource scarcities and ecological stresses constitute real and imminent threats to the future well-being of all people and nations. These challenges are fundamentally non-military and it is imperative that they be addressed accordingly."

Earthscan, a London environmental issues news service, several years ago identified examples where environmental degradation was at least a part of the cause of recent political conflicts:

• Soil erosion and agricultural decline have marginalized millions of peasants in Central America and the Caribbean, causing civil strife there and driving many environmental refugees to the U.S.

• Soil erosion and agricultural decline were involved in the fall of the Shah of Iran, of Emperor Haile Selassie in Ethiopia, of King Zahir in Afghanistan, and in the superpower confrontations that followed.

• Food price increases, another result of sustained neglect of subsistence agriculture, have led to food riots in Brazil, Egypt, Morocco, Tunisia, Zambia, Bolivia, Haiti, and other countries.

• Throughout the Third World, soil erosion is a factor in the migration of subsistence farmers into slums and shantytowns of major cities, producing desperate populations prone to participate in civil violence.

• In the world's drylands, the decreasing agricultural resource base pits nomads against settled farmers. Bloodshed often results.

We are convinced that war and preparation for war is a far greater contributor to current global environmental degradation than is generally realized. We are also convinced that environmental degradation and natural resource depletion is a significant but little recognized cause of political conflict and war.

Earthkeepers' Response

It is the responsibility of Christians through the church and otherwise to work toward the elimination of both war and environmental degradation. The vicious cycle of war leading to environmental degradation and vise versa must be broken if the creation is to be preserved, maintained, and protected. It will take the cooperation and willpower of Christians and all other peoples of the earth for this to happen.

Within the Christian church is both the message for, and the hope of, peacemaking and creation enhancement. It is really the only human institution which will be able to initiate the needed changes.

Several things need to be done in the church to combine peacemaking activities with environmental enhancement:

• The ecumenical church needs to mount a massive educational campaign to inform persons about these issues.

• A biblical creation stewardship theology needs to be rediscovered, reinterpreted, and accepted by all Christians. Both Old Testament and New Testament understandings must be studied, advocated, and accepted.

• Personal spiritual renewal based upon a biblical creation theology—a change of heart—needs to occur. Among other concepts, this personal renewal must recognize that human redemption can be understood only as an integral part of the redemption of the whole creation (Romans 8:18-25).

• This renewal must include personal transformation from status-quo, self-centered, hedonistic, consumptive, and affluent habits toward a lifestyle based on love and concern for the created order, conservation, simplicity, and shalom.

Every spiritually renewed Christian will be able to find some way to work for peace and environmental conservation. Each one's involvement will depend upon specific individual gifts. Personal and corporate participation is essential.

21. What Is Happening to Our Beautiful Land?

Affirmation for our contention that environmental degradation is the number one global problem comes from the Catholic bishops of the Philippines.

In a pastoral letter on ecology entitled "What Is Happening to Our Beautiful Land?" (January 1988), the bishops state their case. In the letter's introduction they say:

> The Philippines is now at a critical point in its history. For the past number of years we have experienced political instability, economic decline, and a growth in armed conflict. . . . The banner headlines absorb our attention so much that we tend to overlook a deep-seated crisis which, we believe, lies at the root of many of our economic and political problems. To put it simply: our country is in peril. All the living systems on land and in the seas around us are being ruthlessly exploited. The damage to date is extensive and sad to say, it is often irreversible.

The Attack on the Natural World

The bishops refer to environmental degradation: deforestation, soil erosion, floods, silting, dried-up river beds, soil erosion and chemical poisoning causing loss of crop yields, shrinking fish catches, and destruction of coral reefs and mangrove forests.

> The picture that is emerging in every province of the country is clear and bleak. The attack on the natural world which benefits very few Filipinos is rapidly whittling away at the very base of our living world and endangering its fruitfulness for future generations.

The bishops describe the exploitation of the natural world as sin, quoting the usual biblical references. They state: "As we reflect on what is happening in the light of the Gospel we are convinced that this assault on creation is sinful and contrary to the teachings of our faith."

The bishops consider environmental degradation a more serious issue than the nuclear threat. In a "call to respect and defend life," they issue a challenge:

> At this point in the history of our country, it is crucial that people motivated by religious faith develop a deep appreciation for the fragility of our islands' life systems and take steps to defend the earth. It is a matter of life and death. We are aware of this threat to life when it comes to nuclear weapons. . . . We tend to forget that the constant, cumulative destruction of life-forms and different habitats will, in the long-term, have the same effect.

The bishops highlight the consequences of environmental destruction. The "scars on nature . . . will mean less nutritious food, poorer health and an uncertain future. This will inevitably lead to an increase in political and social unrest."

The pastoral letter celebrates "the beauty and the pain of the earth." It poetically discusses the forests, seas, continuing variety of creation, deforestation, soil erosion, and deterioration of the seas. The bishops lament the rampant destruction of natural resources of the Philippines in the "name of Progress." "Through our thoughtlessness and greed we have sinned against God and His creation."

In a powerful commentary they say:

> One thing is certain: we cannot continue to ignore and disregard the Earth. Already we are experiencing the consequence of our shortsightedness and folly. Even though we squeeze our lands and try to extract more from them, they produce less food. The air in our cities is heavy with noxious fumes. . . . Our forests are almost gone, our rivers are almost empty, our springs and wells no longer sparkle with living water. During the monsoon rain flash-floods sweep through our town and cities and destroy everything in their path. Our lakes and estuaries are silting up. An out of sight, out of mind mentality allows us to flush toxic waste and mine tailings into our rivers.

Earthkeepers' Response

The bishops appeal to all Filipinos to remember their native heritage and their faith and to begin to reverse the assault on the natural world. They point to "signs of hope," "our vision," and "Christ our life":

> As people of the covenant we are called to protect endangered eco-systems like our forests, mangroves, and coral reefs and to establish just human communities in our land. More and more we must recognize that the commitment to work for justice and to preserve the integrity of creation are two inseparable dimensions of our Christian vocation to work for the kingdom of God in our times. We have much to learn from the attitude of respect which Jesus displayed to the natural world. He was very much aware that all creatures in God's creation are related. Jesus lived lightly on the earth and warned his disciples against hoarding material possessions and allowing their hearts to be enticed by the lure of wealth and power. (Matthew 6:19-21 and Luke 9:1-6)

The pastoral letter concludes with some positive steps that people can take individually, as churches, and as governments. It also points out responsibility that nongovernmental organizations (NGOs) have on these issues:

> NGOs have a very important role to play in developing a wide-spread ecological awareness among people. They can also act as a watch-dog to ensure that the government and those in public office do not renege on their commitment to place this concern at the top of their list.

The letter ends with the familiar biblical passage from Deuteronomy 30:19-20 (adapted): "Today I offer you a choice of life or death, blessing or curse. Choose life, and then you and your descendants will live."

This pastoral letter on ecology, although written for Filipinos, has an important message for all of us. The principles of justice, peace, and integrity of the environment are the same everywhere: in Latin America, Asia, Africa, or North America. The hopeful sign is that there is an increasing understanding by the religious community that environmental degradation is a serious moral and ethical problem. Positive change will occur only as this awareness takes root.

Discussion Questions

1. What are implications when a nation—such as the U.S.—spends more on military-related items than on people programs?

2. As we direct our attention to federal spending that is largely for programs other than human need, what are new ways individuals can be peacemakers in daily living in our communities?

3. Do you agree that the earth cannot support both butter and guns? What must we do individually and politically to reverse this trend?

4. It has been pointed out that war is a force that contributes to environmental destruction and that environmental degradation leads directly to conflict. What can we do to break this destructive cycle? How can peacemaking activities be combined with environmental conservation?

5. It is sometimes easier to see the wrong that others, including nations, do to cause environmental degradation. How can we live individually to promote a more ecologically sound world for the preservation of God's creation and more equitable access to resources for all people?

6. What within your local community contributes to conflict and environmental degradation? How can you address this to stimulate change for the better?

7. Working for change in systems is difficult and frequently results are few and far between. Can you identify others with similar convictions and begin dialogue and activities with a support group?

Resources

For Life: Christian Peacemaking in a Nuclear Age. Slide set, 29 minutes. Available for free loan from MCC Akron, PA 17501; or MCC Canada, 234 Plaza Dr., Winnipeg MB R3T 5K9.

Friesen, Duane K. *Christian Peacemaking and International Conflict.* Scottdale, Pa.: Herald Press, 1986. See pp. 134-141.

Muller, Robert. *A Planet of Hope.* Warwick, N.Y.: Amity House, Inc., 1985.

Peachey, Linda and Titus. "Stages of Conscientious Objection to Military Taxes," MCC U.S. Peace Office, Akron, PA 17501.

Also, *World Peace Begins in Lancaster*. Lancaster County
Peacework Alternatives, 617 S. Lime St., Lancaster, PA 17602.

Sivard, Ruth Leger. *World Military and Social Expenditures 1985*.
Washington, D.C.: World Priorities. Note tables on pp. 33-42.

Sivard, Ruth Leger. *World Military and Social Expenditures 1987-
1988*. Washington, D.C.: World Priorities.

Worldwatch Institute. *State of the World 1986*. New York: W. W.
Norton. Chapter 8, "Harnessing Renewable Energy."

Worldwatch Institute. *State of the World 1987*. New York: W. W.
Norton. Chapter 10, "Designing Sustainable Economies."

"What Is Happening to Our Beautiful Land?" Catholic Bishops of the
Philippines Pastoral Letter. Available from MCC U.S. Global
Education Office, Akron, PA 17501.

Ecology and Economics

However, there should be no poor among you, for in the land the Lord your God is giving you to possess as your inheritance, he will richly bless you, if only you fully obey the Lord your God and are careful to follow all these commands I am giving you today. . . . If there is a poor person among your people in any of the towns of the land that the Lord your God is giving you, do not be hardhearted or tightfisted toward your poor neighbor. Rather be openhanded and freely lend to them whatever they need. . . . Give generously to them and do so without a grudging heart; then because of this the Lord your God will bless you in all your work and in everything you put your hand to. There will always be poor people in the land. Therefore I command you to be openhanded toward your neighbors and toward the poor and needy in your land.
     —Deuteronomy 15:4-11 (adapted for inclusion)

Drought is the result of weather systems,
but desertification is the result of the actions of man.
     —World Food Council Notes

22. Ecology and Modern Economics: In Conflict

Many, if not most, of the problems of environmental degradation discussed in this book are the result of the incompatibility of ecological principles with modern economic systems. There is a built-in conflict between ecology and modern economics. At various places in the book we have referred to the basic concepts of ecology:

- Everything is connected with everything else.
- Everything must go somewhere.
- Nature knows best.
- There is no such thing as a free lunch.

In this chapter we will review and examine these four concepts and suggest how we think they relate to our economic system.

Everything Is Connected

The first of these four ecological principles was coined by Barry Commoner in the book *The Closing Circle*: "Everything is connected with everything else in nature." The physical and biological world is interrelated and must be seen as a whole.

Our economic systems assume that we can isolate ourselves from nature. Nature is a problem to be controlled and dominated. Nature just gets in our way. We solve problems in isolation, dealing with only one part of the natural world at a time. We do not see or want to see the connectedness of one part of the natural world with another.

No More "Away"

The second ecological principle states, "Everything must go somewhere." This is the basic science principle that says that matter can neither be created nor destroyed. Matter (things) must be recycled for nature to be sustained.

Industrial economic systems assume that there will always be an "away" to which things can be thrown. They have little concern about what to do with wastes. This assumption is responsible for the universal problems of landfill siting and waste disposal that have developed in the industrial world today.

God's Creation Is Good

The third ecological principle, "Nature knows best," simply acknowledges the truth of the Creator's comment on the creation: "It is good." It is a balanced ecosystem that is self-regulating and maintaining. Left alone it is sustainable.

Our economic systems assume that human beings with modern science and technology can improve upon nature's systems. We are confident that science will always be able to come up with a technological fix to solve any "problem" that nature presents us with. We do not really pay much attention to how nature works.

No Free Lunch

The fourth ecological principle is one stressed frequently in this book, but much disregarded by our economic systems: "There is no such thing as a free lunch." This is a simple way to say that energy travels a one-way street from the sun through the living world (ecosystem) and is finally lost or made unusable. Energy cannot be recycled like matter can. Therefore, there is no way to get more energy out of a system than is put into it. In fact, there always will be less. This is also called the second law of thermodynamics in the field of bioenergetics.

Our economic system assumes that we can get more out of a system than is put in. The myth of the free (or cheap) lunch permeates industrial society. One can "make money." We can increase productivity without more effort. Work can be painless. We can win the lottery. We can have a continual-growth economy. We can get higher and higher returns with less and less effort. We can get something for nothing. None of these is true. Yet the myth of a free lunch undergirds the world's economic systems.

By using science and technology and exploiting fossil fuels and other natural resources, humankind has been able to postpone the real consequences of the neglect of these ecological principles to this point. But the results are now showing up as the environmental degradation we have described. The modern world has been living on borrowed time. Unless economists—all of us—begin soon to accept the laws of ecology, the environmental bills coming due will only increase. The longer environmental neglect occurs, the more severe the consequences will become.

Earthkeepers' Response

It is not yet too late. What is needed is a return to the stewardship-of-creation theology described in the Bible. Christians must become leaders in rediscovering the biblical design of faith and economics—a system in which economics is again compatible with ecological laws. Such a pattern calls for conserving energy and developing alternate renewable forms, stabilizing the human population, recycling of all materials, protecting and renewing the environment, and developing lifestyles that incorporate these actions.

23. Development and Natural Resources

R. J. Mitchel, in an essay in the book *World Food, Population and Development* (edited by Gigi M. Berardi), defines development as "a process of social, economic, and political change and growth where people's needs for land, food, shelter, education, health care, energy supplies, and improved techniques are methodically being satisfied."

To accomplish this process, development workers are aware of a wide variety of global issues. Many of these issues relate to natural resources and the environment. One of the best related analyses is found in a report of the Global Possible Conference held at Wye, Maryland, in May 1984. The conference was sponsored by the World Resources Institute which was established in late 1982 "to help governments, international organizations, the private sector, and others address a fundamental question: How can we meet basic human needs and nurture economic growth without undermining the natural resources and environmental integrity on which life, economic vitality and international security depend?"

This, we believe, is a crucial question for development workers. How can we best help the 450 million people who are hungry in our world today? How do we help the one billion people whom the World Bank calls the "absolute poor"? How can we assure that all people will have enough physical necessities of life and at the same time not put undue stress on the earth's natural environment and its resources?

The 75 experts and leaders from 20 countries identified the primary issues relative to the above question. Then they developed an "agenda for action" at the Global Possible Conference. We have summarized these objectives because it is an important document for Christians interested in development to help Third-World peoples out of their poverty. Major issues and suggested actions from the *Global Possible Report* follow.

Population, Poverty, and Development

Although worldwide population growth has declined (to 1.7 percent annually), the developing countries of the world, where there is the most poverty, continue to face rapid growth (up to 4 percent annually). To work at this issue, initiatives are needed in three areas: actions to reduce poverty; actions to improve the position and employment of women; and actions to reduce mortality and birth rates. To achieve these goals, Third-World governments and helping agencies (like Mennonite Central Committee) should take the following actions:

• Adopt labor-intensive economic development strategies aimed at alleviating poverty by expanding employment opportunities.

• Reduce death rates by making basic sanitary services and simple health care widely available.

• Expand greatly the educational and employment opportunities for women.

• Set and achieve an international goal of doubling access to family planning services in the Third World over the next decade.

To achieve these goals, the industrialized countries of the world must simplify import procedures, eliminate import restrictions, increase development assistance, and help Third-World countries reduce their debt burdens. For the record, in 1986 Canada was the eighth and U.S. the eighteenth of 18 developed countries in development aid provided to the Third World as a percentage of gross national product (GNP).

Urban Sprawl

By 2000, most of the largest cities will be in the Third World; half of the Third World will be urban. Lower-income groups in these cities already lack space, drinking water, sanitation, and adequate housing.

Policies are needed to slow the rate of migration, decentralize industries, provide employment in rural areas, and help to improve rural living conditions by providing health, education, and other basic services.

Fresh Water

There are areas, regions, and even nations that have experienced (or soon will face) serious water shortages or water pollution. Providing safe drinking water is a major challenge and expense for both developing and industrialized nations. Three water resource goals to work toward are dependable and safe water supplies for people, protection and management of the environmental systems through which water moves, and efficient water use.

Biological Diversity

The maintenance of biological diversity is important for the functioning of natural systems, improvement of crops and livestock, and development of new pharmaceuticals and other useful products. Habitat destruction is causing a historically unprecedented and accelerating loss of genetic resources and extinction of species, particularly in the tropics. To halt this accelerating loss of our genetic heritage, cooperative efforts need to be made by governments, international organizations, and others.

Tropical Forests

In contrast to relatively stable forests in the developed world, the area of forests in the Third World has declined by 50 percent during this century due primarily to agricultural settlement. The principal underlying causes of tropical deforestation include rural poverty, low agricultural productivity, inequalities in land tenure, population pressure, and the lack of integrated planning of forestry agriculture, energy, and other sectors. All these root causes of deforestation must be addressed.

Agricultural Land

Much land currently in agriculture is deteriorating due to inappropriate soil and water management. Loss of topsoil through erosion is the most widespread form of degradation. Other serious problems include salinization, compacting, and waterlogging.

Along with desertification, these reduce productivity and jeopardize long-range sustainability.

Governments and international organizations need to underwrite land policies that promote intensified sustainable production on existing good agricultural lands rather than expanding production to marginal lands. They need to direct their activities toward small landholders, emphasize soil conservation methods, and reduce the impacts of livestock overgrazing on arid and semi-arid lands.

Living Marine Sources

The marine environment plays a central role in the biological, chemical, and physical cycles on which all life depends. Today it is recognized that even though the oceans are vast, their ecological balance can be upset by human activity. To preserve and enhance the harvest of living marine resources, steps such as the following will be needed: improve fishing management, prevent pollution and physical destruction of critical habitats, expand programs to help coastal developing countries effectively manage their shore zones, and assist Third-World countries in aquaculture development.

Energy

With the present world oil glut, it is difficult to realize that sometime in the next 15 to 25 years global oil production will begin to decline as it already has in non-OPEC producing countries. There needs to be a plan for transition from dependence primarily on oil to other sources of energy. The *Global Possible Report* (p. 509) states:

> Conventional energy strategies that focus mainly on fossil fuels and nuclear energy pay insufficient attention to (1) the environmental impacts of expanded fossil fuel use, (2) the threat of nuclear weapons proliferation implicit in widespread nuclear fuel enrichment, (3) the political and economic vulnerability of economies highly dependent on imported energy, (4) the pressing energy needs of the rural sector in developing countries, (5) the economic impact of ex-

panding energy use in the industrial countries on the growth of developing countries, and (6) the imperative to meet the basic human needs of the poor, especially of women and households.

New energy strategies are needed that recognize these challenges. To have a sustainable society, we must promote a sustainable energy supply. The *Global Possible Report* suggests these strategies among others for dealing with the energy issue:

• Promote rapid gains in *conservation* and *energy efficiency* as the highest priority through raising domestic oil and natural gas prices to international levels.

• Promote the development of renewable energy sources, including decentralized solar, wind, hydro, and biomass technologies, by eliminating subsidies to fossil and nuclear supply sources.

• Adopt an oil import levy.

• Insist on control of pollution and other environmental impacts of energy production.

Atmosphere and Climate

Scientific investigations during the past decade point to serious potential changes in the global atmosphere and climate due to human activities. The most serious transnational atmospheric problems that still need to be better understood include acid rain, stratospheric ozone depletion, and the greenhouse effect—climate change caused by the buildup in the atmosphere of carbon dioxide and other gases.

Earthkeepers' Response

To counteract the above problems, the *Global Possible Report* recommends that governments, international organizations, and others should "pursue vigorously three policies: energy conservation and improvements in energy use efficiency, rapid development of renewable energy sources and forest conservation and reforestation. These measures could have positive effects on local air pollution problems, transboundary pollution such as acid deposition, and global issues such as build-up of carbon dioxide."

For a full report of the issues and actions summarized here, the reader is invited to refer to the book, *The Global Possible*. To effectively work at long-term solutions to the problems of hunger and poverty, development workers will need to be aware of the above issues. Programs and projects must reflect an understanding that the environmental and natural resource base upon which development depends is of critical importance to long-term solutions. Appropriate development must give center stage to the earlier question: How can we help meet basic human needs in today's world without undermining the creation by which life is sustained?

24. Ecological Look at World Hunger: Twelve Myths

Frances Moore Lappe and Joseph Collins are considered by many to be among the world's foremost experts on food and agriculture issues. Lappe is the author of the international best seller *Diet For A Small Planet*. With Collins, she founded the San Francisco-based Institute for Food and Development Policy in 1975. They have published many books and articles; *World Hunger: Twelve Myths* was released in 1986.

Here is a summary of those 12 myths, responses by Lappe and Collins, then our comments.

Myth 1: With food-producing resources in so much of the world stretched to the limit, there's simply not enough food to go around. Unfortunately, some people have to go hungry.

Their reply: The world today produces enough grain to provide everyone on earth with 3,600 calories a day. Abundance, not scarcity, best describes the food supply in the world today.

Commentary: While there is enough food produced in the world, if it were evenly distributed, there is a problem with the way much of this food is being produced. The "abundance" today is achieved at the expense of the soil, nonrenewable fuels, and a healthy environment. We're using up the "capital of production" by borrowing natural resources from the future. No one really knows what the "carrying capacity" of the earth is. Complacency about sufficient food production at this time is unwarranted. A sustainable method of food production must s on be implemented worldwide.

Myth 2: Droughts and other events beyond human control cause famine.

Their reply: Clearly, human-made forces are making people increasingly vulnerable to nature's vagaries. Natural events are not the cause—they are the final blow.

Commentary: Natural disasters like drought, flood, and typhoon do not cause chronic hunger by themselves. Their impact is often worsened by human acts contributing to erosion, deforestation, and the greenhouse effect. Also, where food security is already precarious, as in most Third-World countries, a natural catastrophe may make hunger more severe. Famine, though, is basically man-made in today's world.

Myth 3: Hunger is caused by too many people pressing against finite resources. We must slow population growth before we can hope to alleviate hunger.

Their reply: There doesn't seem to be a correlation between population density and hunger. Hunger, the most dramatic symptom of pervasive poverty, and rapid population growth occur together because they have a common cause. By decreasing poverty, population growth will also decrease.

Commentary: Human overpopulation is not a primary cause of hunger—on the contrary, hunger (and poverty) are considered to be a cause of overpopulation. As economic conditions improve for poor people, they feel less need for many children. In the longer term, population will need to be stabilized worldwide. The best way to stabilize population (and to eliminate hunger) is to decrease world poverty.

Myth 4: Pressure to feed the world's hungry is destroying the very resources needed to grow food. Clearly we cannot both feed the hungry and protect our environment.

Their reply: That an environmental crisis is undercutting our food-producing resources is no myth, but myths and half-truths confound our grasp of the root causes of the crisis. We need to ask many questions, including why peasants are denied productive land and forced to farm land subject to environmental degradation, why forests are cut down, and why farmers use chemicals.

Commentary: We can feed the hungry and protect the environment at the same time, but not the way we're trying to do it now. A return to labor-intensive, sustainable agriculture with the recycling of natural resources will be essential. Sadly, this "myth" is already a reality in many parts of the Third World where population pressure is degrading the environment.

Myth 5: The green revolution is the answer. The miracle seeds of the green revolution increase grain yields and therefore are a key to ending world hunger. Now biotechnology offers an even more dramatic food production revolution. More food means less hunger.

Their reply: The first green revolution has increased food production greatly. The second green revolution (biotechnology) is promising. But increasing food production this way has hidden costs. Just because there is more food is no assurance that the hungry poor will eat better—or at all.

Commentary: There simply is no free lunch in nature. Increased food production—with hybrid seeds and chemicals (green revolution I) or with biotechnology and genetic engineering (green revolution II)—has had and will continue to have negative side effects, including loss of wild-type genes and environmental damage. Short-term benefits of this kind of food production will be nullified by long-term consequences.

Myth 6: The big farmers have the know-how to produce better. Even though we want to be fair, reforms that take land away from the big producers will lower food output and therefore hurt the hungry people they are supposed to help.

Their reply: Many big farmers underuse and misuse food resources. The small farmer is almost always more productive than the large landowner. They work their land more intensively.

Commentary: Industrial agriculture may be productive, but it is not energy efficient. American agriculture consumes about 10 calories of energy input for each calorie of food placed on the table. A Chinese rice farmer can produce about 50 calories of food energy for every calorie of energy input. Small farmers are usually better conservationists, too. Land in their hands will benefit the poor.

Myth 7: If governments just got out of the way, the free market could work to alleviate hunger.

Their reply: Such a "market is good/government is bad" formula can never help address the causes of hunger. Every economy on earth combines the market and government in allocating resources and distributing goods.

Commentary: The authors are "right on" here, we believe. We don't think there is such a thing as a totally "free market" economy in our interdependent world today. Thus, how can it be argued that countries with a so-called "free market economy" have fewer hungry people? Other factors are more important.

Myth 8: Free trade is the answer. World trade could reflect the comparative advantage of each country—each exporting what it can produce most cheaply and importing what it cannot.

Their reply: A nice theory. It falls apart in the real world. If increased exports contributed to the alleviation of poverty and hunger, how can we explain that in so many Third-World countries exports have boomed while hunger has grown?

Commentary: Fair (equitable) trade is needed. Again, what is "free trade"? The problem has been and is that the world's financial (political) powers control the "free trade." If free trade were fair, it would certainly be preferable to the "protectionism" being discussed so much at present.

Myth 9: If initiative for change must come from the poor, then the situation truly is hopeless. They can hardly be expected to bring about change.

Their reply: Survival (for the poor) demands resourcefulness and learning the value of joint effort. If the poor were truly passive, few of them could even survive.

Commentary: The poor have plenty to offer. Numerous development projects demonstrate that the poor can initiate change and break the poverty cycle when they are given shared power and provided incentive. The prospect of alleviating poverty is not hopeless, if the poor are given a proper chance.

Myth 10: In helping to end world hunger, our primary responsibility as U.S. citizens is to increase and improve our government's foreign aid.

Their reply: Our primary responsibility as U.S. citizens is to make certain our government's policies are not making it harder for people to end hunger for themselves. Genuine freedom can only be won by people for themselves.

Commentary: The authors are on target here. Most of the foreign aid provided for developing countries by the U.S. government has not gone to help the poor. Recently most of it has gone for military hardware, not food, to support military regimes favorable to the U.S. Some has been returned to multinational corporations for "development" projects. There is a place for government aid to poor countries, but it should be carefully targeted to the poor.

Myth 11: Deep down we know hunger benefits us. Americans would have to sacrifice too much of their standard of living for there to be a world without hunger.

Their reply: The biggest threat to our own well-being is not the advancement of the hungry, but their continued deprivation.

Commentary: Blocking world peace and stability is the present, intolerable rich-poor gap between the developed and developing countries. To decrease this gap, some Americans (and others) will certainly need (and can afford) to lower their unrealistic standards of living. Most people don't think much about this problem, though, as the myth suggests.

Myth 12: Societies that eliminate hunger also end up eliminating the freedoms of their citizens. People may just have to choose one or the other.

Their reply: Taking "freedom" to mean civil liberties, the authors can think of no theoretical or practical reason why it should be incompatible with ending hunger. There are good reasons to expect greater progress toward ending hunger in societies where civil liberties are protected.

Commentary: It depends here on how one defines "freedom." If it means license to exploit in a "free market" economy, then there may be a conflict between "freedom" and ending hunger. That kind of freedom, although rationalized by some people, is in conflict with Christian teachings about care for the poor and oppressed. There is no evidence that ending hunger should conflict with a people's civil liberties.

Earthkeepers' Response

The myths about world hunger are many. There is disagreement about the causes of and solutions to the scandalous problem. Lappe and Collins provide good insight to the problem with their 15 years of study and research on it. They should be taken seriously. Their basic thesis—that hunger is a political problem—has much merit. Their thesis is probably true for the present. However, if the hunger problem is to be addressed fully, we need to give as much attention to the worldwide ecological problem of sustainable food production for a rapidly growing human population and the associated environmental degradation.

Christians are called to love God, the creation, and their neighbors. We are challenged today to sort out the important issues related to world hunger and respond in every appropriate way to eliminate it. We do not believe that God wills any of his people to be hungry.

Discussion Questions

1. Describe in your own words each of the "laws of ecology" suggested by Barry Commoner. Explain how each conflicts with an accepted economic assumption.

2. Review elements needed for a system of economics that is more compatible with the laws of ecology (see end of chapter 22). How can these and others be implemented? What can you do to help?

3. Read the fundamental question on development stated in the second paragraph of chapter 23. Do you think it is a valid question? Explain. Give some general answers to the question.

4. Discuss the question of urbanization as it relates to development and natural resources? Should urbanization be reversed? How?

5. Define each issue listed in chapter 23. How is each a moral question? What is Christian responsibility in the face of these circumstances?

6. Examine each hunger "myth" in the article by Lappe and Collins. Interpret each one and compare with the commentary given. To what extent do you agree with each myth and commentary?

Resources

Berardi, Gigi M., ed. *World Food, Population, and Development.* Lanham, Md.: Rowman and Allanheld, 1986. See essay by R. J. Mitchel.

Edge of Survival. A 60-minute 16mm film on hunger and development. Basic principles relate to this section. Available for free loan from MCC, Akron, PA 17501.

Hunger. Ten-minute slide set. Part I, *Hunger, Where and Why,* supplements the hunger myths article. Available for free loan from MCC, Akron.

Lappe, Frances M., and Joseph Collins. *World Hunger: Twelve Myths.* New York: Grove Press, Inc., 1986. Relates to chapter 24.

Kreider, Carl. *The Rich and the Poor—A Christian Perspective on Global Economics.* Scottdale, Pa.: Herald Press, 1987. A good general reference on this subject.

Repetto, Robert, ed. *The Global Possible: Resources, Development and the New Century.* New Haven: Yale University Press, 1985. Provides details for chapter 23.

Schumacher, E. F. *Small Is Beautiful: Economics As If People Mattered.* New York: Harper and Row, 1973. A classic on responsible economics.

Population Pressures

Happy are those who have reverence for the Lord,
who live by his commands.
Your work will provide for your needs;
you will be happy and prosperous.
A man who obeys the Lord
will surely be blessed like this.
        —Psalm 128:1-2, 4 (TEV)

25. Population Passes Five Billion Mark

Over five billion people now inhabit our planet! The Population Institute, a Washington-based private research organization, estimated that on 7 July 1986, the five billionth person was born. Other research groups have generally agreed with that estimate.

How many is five billion? Imagine individuals passing by you, one each second, day and night continually. It would take over 158 years for 5 billion people to pass by in this way. That's a lot of people.

Five billion, the actual number, is hard to fathom. But the rate at which the human population has grown and is growing is even more so. It took thousands of years for world population to reach one billion in 1850. By 1950 it had more than doubled. In the past 100 years, population has tripled. It is expected to double to 10 billion in another 34 to 40 years.

One million people are added to the earth every four to five days, 85 million each year. Eighty percent of this rapid population growth is occurring in the Third World, where the population is doubling every 20 to 25 years there.

There are two main reasons for recent rapid population growth: death rate reduction and increased energy availability to supply food. Living populations are limited by environmental factors such as lack of food, water, natural resources, space, and pollution. Through use of science and technology, primarily in medicine and agriculture, humans have been able to circumvent (postpone) these limitations imposed by nature to this point. How long this can continue is an open question.

Carrying Capacity

Some scientists think that earth's carrying capacity—the population an area will support without undergoing deterioration —has already been reached. The executive director of Population-Environment Balance, M. Rupert Cutler, says, "Five billion (people) probably puts the world population about at its carrying capacity. It will be difficult to feed, clothe, shelter, and employ many more people at more than a subsistence level of life."

Population Institute President Werner Fornos states that "while the numbers (5 billion) are staggering the consequences of such startling growth are even more so. The child (the 5 billionth) very probably will be born in the Third World where nine of ten babies are born today and where poverty, disease, hunger, illiteracy, and unemployment make life a daily struggle for survival."

How many people can the earth support? It depends upon many factors, such as where they are willing to live and at what level of subsistence. We believe there is good evidence that the earth is not far from reaching the carrying capacity that Cutler and Fornos suggest. It is clear that present rates of population growth and natural resource consumption are unsustainable.

Two things are needed if the good earth that God entrusted to us is to be sustained: human population stabilization and natural resource control.

How can population be stabilized? In poor countries children are seen to be a source of income and security. Most studies show that the number of children born in a family is related to its socioeconomic level. So an appropriate way to help stabilize population is to empower the poor. Programs of community and economic development combined with education and locally controlled family planning are ways to work. Mission, relief, and development agencies are equipped to do this best. The Mennonite Central Committee (MCC) Hillsboro Resolution on the World

Food Crisis (1974 and 1984) states the principle well. It recommends "that MCC expand our efforts toward projects and advocacy for the very poor. This will include research and extension programs emphasizing increased food production, more employment opportunities, population stabilization, and appropriate technology."

What about natural resource control? Though it is clear that overpopulation (primarily in the Third World) is placing undue stress on the earth's carrying capacity, it should be emphasized that overconsumption of natural resources by the rich is as much or more responsible. This is illustrated by a simulated conversation in cartoon form between a rich person and a poor person. It goes like this:

Rich person: Do you realize that the world's population is going to double in 35 years? What are you going to do about that?

Poor person: What's wrong with people? I like people.

Rich person: Well, so do I, of course. But the world's resources can't support an ever-increasing population—don't you see?

Poor person: I see. So it's a matter of resources, as well as people. Do you realize that the richest 10 percent of earth's people consume about 90 percent of the world's resources? What are you going to do about that?

Earthkeepers' Response

Responsibility for earth stewardship is thus seen as shared between rich and poor. The poor must share in some response to the overpopulation concern. The rich must respond to the overconsumption concern.

Today, we believe, there are enough resources on the earth to meet the needs of five billion people without degrading the environment. These resources are not being equitably shared, however, and future availability is in question. Christians, who desire to demonstrate love for the Creator, the earth, and their neighbors, will need to do a better job of earth stewardship. In this way world population can be stabilized and natural resources conserved. Both conditions are essential if we are to live fulfilled lives in a sustainable world as the Lord intended.

26. Urban In-migration and Ecology

The Scene in Haiti and Central America

One consequence of hunger, poverty, and environmental degradation in the rural Third World is the increasing migration of poor people to already overcrowded cities. In 1988 we visited Haiti and four Central American countries on an MCC study trip. The negative impact of this immigration was dramatically apparent there, especially in the cities of Port-au-Prince, San Salvador, and Tegucigalpa.

It was encouraging to see that MCC development programs in these countries are focusing on projects to enhance rural living, to help people remain on the land and become more self-reliant. These programs aim to slow down or reverse the disastrous trend of migration to the urban areas. Even in North America, rampant urbanization is neither good nor sustainable. In undeveloped countries, the ill effects are more quickly noticed.

The growth of cities, particularly in the Third World, is a recent event in history. Lester Brown writes in *State of the World 1987*:

> As recently as 1900 fewer than 14 percent of the world's people lived in cities. . . . The number of people living in cities increased from 600 million in 1950 to over 2 billion in 1986. At the current rate of growth (2.5 percent annually), the number of people living in cities throughout the world will double in the next 28 years. Nearly nine-tenths of this growth will occur in the Third World where the annual urban growth rate is 3.5 percent. (Cities there will double in size in just 20 years.) Aside from the growth of world population itself, urbanization is the dominant demographic trend of the late twentieth century.

From *Gaia: An Atlas of Planet Management* are these comments: "Every day an estimated 75,000 poor people, hoping for work, stream in from rural areas to overwhelm city services and administration. The majority of newcomers head for the barrios, favelas, and shantytowns—made from corrugated iron, plastic sheets and packing cases—which now ring the outskirts of most [Third-World] cities."

Haiti

San Martin, a section of Port-au-Prince, Haiti, illustrates this process well. San Martin is a shantytown just one square mile in area that houses 100,000 people. Most are economic refugees from the environmentally degraded countryside of Haiti. The substandard housing and incredible population density of San Martin produces intolerable living conditions. An open sewage canal (financed by the World Bank) traverses the community. As might be expected it is filled with garbage and debris, which adds to the degradation of the area. Sanitation and water supply are totally inadequate. People are hungry.

In San Martin, Mennonite Economic Development Associates (MEDA) works with small business persons attempting to bring some hope to the stressed community. Both MCC and MEDA programs in Haiti are appropriate and appreciated. However, long-term solutions lie in rural development. MCC aims to make living in the country more attractive so people will not be so tempted to move to the city.

Lester R. Brown observes:

> The present uncontrolled urban growth in the Third World is the result of failed economic and population policies driven more by rural poverty than urban prosperity. . . . For developing nations the policy of neglecting agriculture has produced stagnating or inadequate income growth in rural areas while the policy of importing large scale labor-saving technology to achieve instant industrialization has meant that urban job opportunities have not grown as fast as the numbers seeking work.

Central America

Cities need large quantities of food, water, and fuel far beyond what nature can normally provide. Waste output of a city creates stress on the land and water supply. (Managua, Nicaragua, was the only major city on our trip where the city water supply was said to be "fit to drink.") Air pollution from vehicles, cooking fires, and industry was severe in most of the cities we visited. Garbage, filth, debris, and open sewers were prevalent in all the poor sections of cities visited.

Lawyer Oscar Puerto, vice president of a Honduras human rights organization, described for our group the problems of migration from country areas to Tegucigalpa.

> Twenty-five new people arrive (on average) each day. The city simply cannot absorb that many. Fifty-five percent of the population of Tegucigalpa already live in slums. There is an unemployment rate of 33 percent. But it is not surprising that rural people still want to come to the city. One hundred and fifty thousand rural Honduran families are landless; 60 percent are illiterate; 36 percent of school-aged children are not in school. Honduras has only 1,300 medical doctors and 536 nurses (mostly in the city) for a population of nearly five million.

The reasons why rural Third-World people want to move to the city are obvious. But as Puerto says, cities are just not able to absorb them. It takes a large amount of imported energy for an urban society to exist with a decent standard of living. For example, in the U.S.—a highly urbanized society—of the total energy used in the food system alone, one-third is used in food production, one-third in transporting, processing, and distribution, and one-third in preparing it.

As Third-World cities and societies urbanize, they will require increased amounts of energy for food, fuel, and waste management. From where will that energy come? How will it be financed? It is clear that urban dwellers in the Third World, as in North America, require more energy than their rural counterparts to achieve the same standard of living. For this and many other reasons, it is important that rural people in the Third World and elsewhere be encouraged to remain rural.

Earthkeepers' Response

We were pleased to find that MCC development programs in Haiti and Central America in cooperation with the Mennonite churches are doing just that. From the excellent agricultural work in Haiti and Guatemala; to the work with cooperatives in Honduras, El Salvador, and Nicaragua; the rural health clinics in Guatemala, Haiti, and El Salvador; and the appropriate technology programs (especially in Guatemala), MCC workers are engaged in rural development that makes rural living more viable. That is significant work in combating one of the root causes of conflict in Central America.

27. Haitian Boat People As Environmental Refugees

A *Christian Science Monitor* article (20 May 1988) reports that Haiti's poor "are fleeing the country in record numbers." Speculation is that they are "political refugees" since the departure of dictator Jean-Claude Duvalier in 1986 and the aborted "elections" of November 1987. The U.S. government calls Haitian migrants "economic refugees."

But these people are neither political nor economic refugees in my view. They are environmental refugees.

According to the *Monitor* article, "Rickety boats are leaving Haiti more frequently than at any time since the massive unchecked surge of migration in 1980 and 1981." The Haitian boat people are also being picked up and returned in record numbers.

Nine months after the Haitian elections, nearly 4,000 Haitians had been returned to Haiti by foreign governments. That number nearly matches the 4,117 returned during the whole fiscal year of 1985-86, a high year according to Jonel Charles, a Haitian Red Cross official.

Because the U.S. calls the migrants "economic refugees," they can legally intercept them and return them to Haiti. Human rights groups say the Haitian migrants are "political refugees." Jean-

Jacques Hornorat, a Haitian human rights activist, and other observers say the "massacre of Haitian voters during last November's elections quashed the hopes of many for a better life and may have spurred more Haitian migrations."

But we believe the cause of the political repression and economic poverty of the Haitian people is the devastating destruction of their natural environment. Haiti is a microcosm of an overpopulated, environmentally degraded earth. It demonstrates graphically what can (and will) happen where there are too many people for limited natural resources.

The colonial powers and multinational corporations, in collusion with the local elite, have exploited this land and its people mercilessly in the past. They continue to extract the last traces of natural resources (timber, charcoal, minerals, cattle grazing) from the land.

Haiti was once a tropical paradise, rich in land and natural resources. Thirty-two percent of its land was arable, compared with 14 percent worldwide. It had abundant rainfall and some minerals. But colonial powers and multinationals seeking wealth and peasants seeking fuel and land for survival have destroyed the environment.

As one travels through Haiti, as the authors did in February 1988, it is overwhelming to see the destruction of forests and land. Forests are gone and are replaced by deserts. Rain water is not retained; rushing water on steep hillsides erodes soil, forming ugly gullies. Reservoirs fill up with silt.

Tropical rain-forest soil is fragile. The 513 people living in each square mile in Haiti continue to cut down the last vestiges of the remaining forest. In the Haitian countryside, the stacks of bagged charcoal beside the road waiting to be hauled to the city for urban cookstoves are a depressing sight.

Without forests, arable land, and water resources, the base of Haiti's economy is gone. In the past Haitians moved to the cities as the rural environment was degraded. There they found increased misery. To control these desperate and disillusioned people, political repression increased. Without food and employment, hunger and poverty escalated.

Earthkeepers' Response

The church is called to aid the hungry, the poor, the powerless. Often this aid has been simply handouts along with an evangelical message. Haiti has many evangelical churches and groups doing such work, including 27 varieties of Mennonites. But evangelism and charity in Haiti are not enough.

Even the combined impact of the excellent forestry, community development, and job-creation work of Mennonite Economic Development Associates (MEDA), Mennonite Central Committee (MCC), and other mission groups is inadequate when measured against the massive need to restore Haiti's environment.

Soil renewal, reforestation, and water development are greatly needed. Education for survival in a regenerated environment is crucial.

The international community must help regenerate the environment if Haiti is to survive as a place of habitation. Some underpopulated countries might accept Haitian population overflow until the local environment recovers. Multinational and governmental exploitation of natural resources must be curtailed. And lessons learned from the abuse of Haiti's environment should motivate us to reexamine our own environmental ethics as we care for our part of God's creation.

Discussion Questions

1. Review the extent of and reasons given for the rapid human-population growth in recent years. Do you agree with this interpretation?

2. Define *carrying capacity*. How many people do you think the earth can hold?

3. It says in Genesis 1:28, "Have many children, so that your descendants will live all over the earth and bring it under their control" (TEV). How do you correlate this with overpopulation and carrying-capacity problems of today?

4. Which is most detrimental to the health of the natural environment, overpopulation or overconsumption? Explain.

5. How do you explain rapid population growth in the Third World and slow growth in the first world?

6. Why do some authorities argue for Americans to have more children? Are you surprised that they have been taken seriously?

7. In your setting, what is an appropriate Christian perspective on population issues?

Resources

Berardi, Gigi M., ed. *World Food, Population, and Development.* Lanham, Md.: Rowman and Allenheld, 1986. Part 2 has nine articles on population issues.

Repetto, Robert. *Population, Resources, Environment: An Uncertain Future.* Population Reference Bureau bulletin, July 1987. Includes 21 color slides to illustrate the issues. PRB Circulation Dept., P.O. Box 96152, Washington, DC 20090-6152.

Worldwatch Papers: Lester R. Brown. *Population Policies for a New Economic Era* (Paper 53); Judith Jacobson. *Promoting Population Stabilization* (54); Lester Brown and Jodi L. Jacobson. *Our Demographically Divided World* (74); Jodi L. Jacobson. *Environmental Refugees: A Yardstick of Habitability* (86). Worldwatch Institute, 1776 Mass. Ave. NW, Washington, DC 20036.

PART FOUR

Food and Energy

Genetic Engineering and World Hunger

Two things I ask of you;
  do not deny them to me before I die:
Remove far from me falsehood and lying;
  give me neither poverty nor riches;
  feed me with the food that I need,
or I shall be full, and deny you,
  and say, "Who is the Lord?"
or I shall be poor, and steal,
  and profane the name of my God.
      —Proverbs 30:7-9 (NRSV)

In one sense biotechnology (genetic engineering) is a double edged sword for the Third World. It has the potential to increase the quality and efficiency of agricultural production. . . . But it also has the potential to disrupt local agriculture and encourage further dependency on expensive agricultural imports and technology. . . . In many ways it depends on who controls and dispenses this new technology. If it is vested primarily in the hands of advanced nations and major businesses, those interests will be in a position to pull the plug on locally significant kinds of agricultural development in the Third World, possibly with dire consequences for national economies and international trading patterns.
      —Jack Doyle in *Multinational Monitor* (28 February 1986)

28. Can Genetic Engineering Solve the World Food Crisis?

There are many proposals to combat hunger and poverty in our world today. Recent spectacular developments in biotechnology have prompted some observers to suggest that genetic engineering—human manipulation of plant and animal genetic material—has the dramatic potential to eliminate hunger. Not everyone agrees.

Biotechnical Revolution

Just what is this biotechnical revolution with its genetic engineering? What are its potential benefits? And what are its costs? Can it really help eliminate world hunger?

In 1952, with grant funds from the Atomic Energy Commission, geneticist James Watson and colleague Francis Crick discovered the molecular structure of a cellular nuclear compound called DNA (deoxyribonucleic acid). DNA was found to be the "gene," the determiner of heredity in living organisms. This discovery opened up a new era in genetic research.

In the 1970s, molecular biologists Herbert Boyer and Stanley Cohen took some genetic material—a piece of DNA—from two unrelated species of microbes and spliced them together, creating a new form of life on a molecular level. The process, called recombinant DNA, is behind what is termed today the "Age of Biotechnology."

According to a 1984 Office of Technology Assessment Report, biotechnology includes "any technique that uses living organisms (or parts of organisms) to make or modify products to improve plants and animals, or to develop microorganisms for specific uses."

The terms *biotechnology, genetic engineering,* and *recombinant DNA* are used interchangeably. In the broadest sense, biotechnology describes both old and new techniques for manipulating organisms for specific purposes. For thousands of years, traditional plant and animal breeding involved genetic selection and cross-fertilization. With the recent understanding of DNA and the genetic code, biotechnology includes gene splicing and transfer, cloning, and other types of bioengineering. The potential for developing new kinds of living organisms now goes far beyond traditional plant and animal breeding.

Effects of Genetic Engineering

Genetic engineering, according to many observers, promises to revolutionize agriculture, food processing, pollution and waste management, energy generation, chemical and pharmaceutical development and production, as well as plant and animal breeding. New genetically engineered cereal crops may be developed to feed a hungry world. New breeds of super animals may be cloned to dramatically increase beef production. One writer talks about the possible development of a cow the size of a small elephant that could produce over 45,000 pounds of milk per year. Microbes may be developed to eat up oil spills, decompose toxic wastes, and fight natural insect pests in the field.

Jeremy Rifkin, head of the Foundation On Economic Trends (based in Washington, D.C.) and an observer of biotechnology, describes the "revolution" in his recent book, *Declaration of A Heretic*:

> Recombinant DNA [genetic engineering] signals the most radical change in our relationship with the natural world since the dawn of

the Age of Pyrotechnology [fire]. . . . With recombinant DNA technology it is now possible to snip, insert, stitch, edit, program and produce new combinations of living things just as our ancestors were able to heat, burn, melt and solder together various inert materials creating new shapes, combinations and forms.

The envisioned potential of genetic engineering has captured the imagination of the business world. By 1984 more than 300 companies had been formed exclusively for biotechnical research and development. Commercial interest in the field was greatly intensified in 1980 after a ruling by the U.S. Supreme Court that genetically altered microbes could be patented.

But can genetic engineering really do what is envisioned? Should it? Can it help solve the hunger problem?

Dangers in Biotechnology

There are problems with this new technology—some serious ones. First, how will genetically engineered organisms adapt to the natural environment into which they may be released, either accidentally or voluntarily? No one knows. It is known that in the past some organisms that have been introduced from one region of the earth to another have caused significant environmental problems; examples are the gypsy moth, Dutch elm disease, starlings, the Japanese beetle, dandelions, and the Mediterranean fruit fly. Second, how will fast-growing genetically engineered cereal crops affect the soil base into which they are placed?

The goal of many projects is a plant or animal with increased food-producing ability. Rifkin says that "the great underlying myth of the Biotechnical Revolution is that it is possible to accelerate the production of more efficient living utilities without ever running out." But can production be accelerated without adverse consequences?

As an example of the above, a cereal plant may be engineered to absorb greater sunlight and increase the rate at which the plant makes food. But increased photosynthesis would also require increased use of soil nutrients. The faster the rate of food-making, the faster the nutrient depletion and the greater the erosion potential of the soil base. Says Rifkin, "Genetic engineering will unquestionably result in short term acceleration of biological materials into useful economic products, but at the expense of depleting the reservoir of life-support materials that are essential for maintaining the reproductive viability of living organisms in the future. In nature there is no such thing as a free lunch!"

Current industrial-agriculture systems in developed countries and similar green-revolution techniques in the Third World also have essentially neglected the "no free lunch" rule. Side effects from this kind of agriculture constitute an enormous "environmental debt," with steadily mounting payments due in the areas of soil erosion, pollution, and nonrenewable resource depletion.

Genetic engineering has the real potential of beginning a second green revolution. In that case, present industrial agricultural's unsustainable activities will be greatly speeded up, with ensuing negative environmental consequences. Rifkin states it well: "All great technological revolutions secure the present by mortgaging the future. . . . Genetic engineering raises the interest rates that will have to be paid by future generations beyond anything we've ever experienced in the long history of our attempts to control the forces of nature."

Earthkeepers' Questions

The use of genetic engineering to help solve the world's hunger problem seems at first thought to be attractive. To question its appeal is not popular. Who would not desire faster, more efficient food production? But, as we have shown before, there is a long-term price to pay when technology circumvents the laws of nature.

In addition, today there are already mountains of cereal grain piled up in the Western world that are not being used to feed the hungry. What is to assure that more food produced by genetic engineering techniques will be used to feed the hungry?

There are many additional questions about biotechnology as it relates to other areas, such as: biological warfare, medical genetics, and control of new organisms by the wealthy and powerful. In an age when the scientific worldview seems to be today's faith system, Christians need to take a closer look at creation technology issues such as genetic engineering.

29. Ecology and Hunger: The Role of Wild Genes

Feeding the five billion people on earth today is a challenge not being fully met. To keep ahead of increasing population, modern agricultural scientists must develop and maintain new crop varieties to counteract new diseases and pests that continue to arise.

The raw material for crop improvement is the seed, the reserve of genetic variability. Genes within the seed are the determiners of characteristics that allow the plant to be successful. Plant breeders' methods are cross-fertilization and selection of improved plant types. Wild genetic resources are responsible for much past crop improvement; they will be increasingly important in the future. All of our major agricultural crops have their origin in natural, wild-type plants. It will be increasingly essential to use these wild genes to keep new crop varieties viable.

The use of wild plants and animals for domestication is as old as humankind. The understanding of genes has occurred only since about 1900, when the science of genetics had its origin.

Taming the Genes

The use of genetic resources in agriculture has been the most far-reaching application of genetics. In the 45 years between 1930 and 1975, U.S. crop yields per acre rose dramatically: corn, 320 percent; potatoes, 311 percent; peanuts, 295 percent; cotton, 188 percent; sugarcane, 141 percent; rice, 117 percent; wheat, 115 percent; and soybeans, 112 percent. About 50 percent of each of these increases can be attributed to the use of genetic resources.

The use of wild genes in crop improvement is significant.

• Wheat, rice, barley, and corn, which make up about 90 percent of world grain production, have all been improved by use of wild genes.

• Wheat's wild relatives have genes for drought resistance, winter hardiness, heat tolerance, higher productivity, increased protein content, and other desirable traits.

Rice gets its resistance to blast and grassy-stunt virus—two of four major diseases of rice in Asia—from a wild rice species. After checking 6,723 samples of wild-type rice, the resistance gene was discovered. Had not that one species of wild rice been collected and stored in a gene bank, the grassy-stunt virus that used to destroy thousands of acres of rice annually would still abound.

Other crops improved by wild genes include potatoes (remember the Irish potato famine?), cassava, sweet potatoes, sunflower, oil palm, cane and beet sugar, cocoa, and cotton. The tomato could not be grown as a commercial crop today without the genetic support of its wild relatives. Lettuce, currants, raspberries, and blackberries have all been improved by wild genes.

The number of crops drawing on wild genetic resources is increasing. The more important the crop, the greater the breeding effort and the greater the likelihood that genes from the wild will be used successfully.

By far the most important use of wild genes has been to develop disease-resistant plants. Other characteristics that may be obtained include pest resistance, high yield, vigor, environmental adaptation, and vitamin improvement. The potential of wild genetic resources for the future is in three main areas: the culture of biochemicals for fuels, the development of new domestic varieties, and the improvement of existing varieties. Breeders and genetics engineers can devise more and more ingenious ways to use available genes, such as gene splicing, but they cannot create new ones. That is why conservation of present wild genetic resources is of utmost importance for the future.

Thirty plants give the world 95 percent of its nutrition, and eight of them provide 75 percent of the total calorie intake. All 30 plants were first cultivated in the Third World. In that sense, the developed Northern Hemisphere is grain rich but gene poor. The developed world depends on Third-World wild genes to maintain productivity and prevent crop devastation.

Shrinking Gene Pool

Since all of our major agricultural crops have their origins in the tropics or subtropics, the primitive indigenous varieties of these regions are the major source of genetic variability today. These varieties are being displaced by more uniform, high-yielding varieties developed in the North. At the same time, wild relatives of crop species prized for their genetic qualities are being lost by rapid deforestation, industrialization, and urbanization in the Third World.

This is why Paul Erlich, well-known American biologist, says, "Aside from nuclear war, there is probably no more serious environmental threat than the continued decay of the genetic variability of crops."

Harold Koopowitz, in *Plant Extinction: A Global Crisis,* says that "by the year 2000 the earth will have lost 40,000 plant species." *The Global 2000 Report to the President* states that half to two-thirds of these species extinctions will result from clearing or degradation of tropical forests.

The main cause of loss of species and thus loss of wild genetic resources is clearly destruction of habitat and overexploitation. Overgrazing threatens wild gene pools of corn, wheat, oats, and sorghum. Urban and agricultural expansion and other changes in land use are threatening wild oats and wheat. Deforestation and irrigation have destroyed some wild rice varieties. All of the tomato's wild relatives have limited distribution, making them extremely vulnerable to habitat destruction.

Conservation of Genetic Resources

In recent years there have been calls to formalize the rights and responsibilities of nations concerning the conservation and exchange of genetic resources. Three reasons are given:

• There is a belief that developing countries are being treated inequitably. They have most of the genetic resources, but the industrialized countries are the only ones with money, research, and development skills to make use of those resources.

• Some countries have started imposing restrictions on the movement of germ plasm, and others are threatening to do likewise. Ethiopia has banned the export of wild coffee. Some African countries are not sending oil palms to Brazil.

• Genetic resources are being patented. The use of resources is now big business, and companies want to own the resources they use. Transnational drug, chemical, and petroleum industries are buying heavily into the seed industry. Major buyers are corporations, such as Shell, Pfizer, Upjohn, and ARCO.

Whether international regulation of genetic material can be established and whether it can effectively address these concerns are open questions.

Earthkeepers' Response

Much needs to be done if we are to reverse the trend toward accelerating genetic loss. Of great importance is the reversal of habitat destruction. Environmental preserves and gene banks are needed to preserve remaining wild resources. An environmental preserve can maintain wild species. A gene bank can preserve the germ plasm in the form of seeds, pollen, ova, or plant parts.

Under the auspices of the U.N. Food and Agriculture Organization, a network of 38 centers storing 30 crop genes has been developed. More are needed. There has been less success in protecting wild genes in parks and preserves. Fewer than 15 percent of countries around the world permit the collection of genetic resources in their parks and reserves.

The plant genetic resources of the Third World are the vital ingredients that keep us eating. Seeds are the first link in the food chain. Their protection, preservation, and international control are essential to continue to feed the world.

30. Patents and Genetic Engineering

The U.S. Patent Office in 1988 granted a patent for a genetically engineered animal, a mouse with a spliced-in gene that causes breast cancer. On the same day that the news media announced this first animal patent, Art heard Cary Fowler, codirector of the Rural Advancement Fund International, speak on the topic "Biotechnology and the Agribusiness System's Promises and Problems." Fowler is one of a few generalist scholars who have studied biotechnology and genetic engineering intensely. He was speaking at the annual sessions of Agricultural Missions, Incorporated, a development agency of mainline churches.

Though the media paid little attention to the announcement of this first animal patenting, Fowler and others say it is a vitally important development. The decision to patent animals has ethical, social, and economic implications. It raises many questions. Do humans have the right to so drastically modify created organisms at such a basic level, physically removing genes from one species and putting them into another? What about modifying the human genotype with genes from other species, a distinct possibility now? Who has the right to patent living things at all? Who benefits? Who is harmed? Who will control the process?

The patenting of living things began in the U.S. in 1930 with the Plant Patenting Act, which cover such things as fruit trees and strawberries. In 1970 the Plant Variety Protection Act was passed to protect crop plants like corn, wheat, and soybeans. In 1980 a Supreme Court decision allowed the first patenting of genetically engineered microorganisms. Now patenting of such animals has begun. The next step advocated by some is the patenting of individual genes. Examples are genes for drought tolerance, for disease resistance, and for protein content.

Promises and Pitfalls

Some individuals and groups have questioned this "progression of patenting" all along. They question the granting of legal control over the material substances of food production to private interests for extended periods of time. They believe people need more time to study the implications of patenting organisms, particularly as it relates to genetic engineering. Several bills in the U.S. Congress would allow more time to study these issues before granting more animal patents.

What are some of the promises and pitfalls of genetic engineering? Here are several examples reviewed by Fowler:

- Genetically engineered microbes that will produce vanilla have been developed. This vanilla is identical to that produced by vanilla beans. It is possible that several large vanilla-producing factories could soon supply the whole world with vanilla. Farmers in Madagascar (70,000 of them) and elsewhere who now grow vanilla beans as their primary cash crop could be out of business were this to happen.

- Genetic engineering in cocoa production may increase plant efficiency by 750 percent. Palm oil production could increase by 500 percent with the new techniques. Most cocoa and palm oil producers are small Third-World farmers. To use the new techniques will necessitate large operations. What will happen to the small producers?

- A berry that is 100,000 times as sweet as sugar has been found in Africa. Potentially via genetic engineering this plant has the potential to replace cane and beet sugar. The present sugar industry, already in trouble, would suffer disaster.

- It is predicted that organisms that cause African sleeping sickness in cattle (trypanosomes) may be eliminated through genetic engineering techniques. If this disease were controlled, much more of the vast continent of Africa could be used to raise cattle. Might Africa become the center of world beef production? What would be the consequences for present beef farmers elsewhere?

- Genetic engineering is now being used in research on biological warfare. The U.S. government had explored it in the 1950s. But the possibility that such weapons could be used in retaliation on the identifiable perpetrator, made further development unthinkable. Thus President Nixon signed a bill to outlaw biological weapons. With genetic engineering now available, it is possible to develop microbes that can be better controlled. Special microbes are being developed that could be used secretly to destroy a country's cotton, corn, or bean crop without fear of retaliation. Thus, since 1980, the United States has revived research in biological weaponry. A 900-percent increase in such funding has provided over $400 million for it since 1980.

There are many other concerns about the gene revolution. Comparisons between it and the earlier green revolution—when chemicals were introduced to industrial agriculture—illustrate these concerns:

- The green revolution developed largely with public financial support, whereas the gene revolution is being funded privately.
- The green revolution concentrated on basic cereal crop plants like corn, rice, wheat, and soybeans, while the gene revolution can be applied to all living things.
- The green revolution occurred gradually over 35 to 40 years, but the gene revolution is occurring explosively.
- The green revolution involved about 200 sponsors; the gene revolution already has over 5,000 sponsors with a $12 billion investment, all awaiting for their profit.

The economic potential of genetic engineering has attracted vast amounts of money, spurred many scientists, and led to many corporate marriages. More than 1,000 independent seed companies have been bought out by petrochemical and pharmaceutical companies in the last few years. Research and marketing a new chemical is estimated to cost about $40 million. But if petrochemical companies can genetically engineer a plant to be pesticide resistant and then patent it, they will likely be able to profitably market both plant and pesticide as a package. Seventy companies are working now on such pesticide-resistant plant varieties.

Earthkeepers' Questions

Genetic engineering is complex but understandable. It is a two-edged sword. It has potential for good but also for harm. Its explosive development should not be left to a few scientists, financiers, and government officials. It is sure to have far-reaching effects on agriculture and food systems in both the industrialized world and the Third World.

The recent patenting of animal life also raises more serious questions as to who will benefit. To those who have studied the consequences of the green revolution and previous plant patenting, up to now the answer is clear—those who will benefit most are the already rich and powerful. It is unclear who will pay the price, economically and environmentally.

31. Biotechnology: An Issue the Church Must Face

The age of biotechnology is here. Public concern about the ramifications of this technology is intensifying. The media has discovered some of the profound implications for good or ill of biotechnology. But the church has not yet adequately addressed the moral and ethical issues of this rapidly escalating technology.

In a column in *Catholic Rural Life* (November 1987), Walt Grazer reports on a symposium on biotechnology. He said U.S. Congressional Representative George Brown, chairperson of the House agriculture subcommittee on biotechnology regulation, advised scientists attending the symposium "to be more directly engaged in the legislative process [on biotechnology] or lose their capacity to help shape the issue."

Grazer then suggests that Brown's advice to the scientists is equally good advice to the church. With that we strongly concur.

Jack Doyle, author and director of the Biotechnology Project for the Environmental Policy Institute, writes that "biotechnology is unlike any technology that has preceded it, brimming with good or ill. Here is a technology as powerful as the splitting of the atom or as significantly new and revolutionary in a techno-gadget sense as the transistor or the microchip."

Biotechnology, an Information Revolution

Doyle describes biotechnology as a "fundamental information revolution" and compares it with the invention of the printing press, but with far greater reach. "The most important thing about biotechnology is that it is a technology of control, the center of which is DNA (deoxyribonucleic acid) the universal substance of life itself," says Doyle.

The proliferation of genetic engineering in the past two decades has touched many areas. It involves gene manipulations and uses a variety of sophisticated techniques to do this. One is called gene splicing. The gene (a bit of DNA) from one species of organism is spliced into a virus or bacterium which acts as the medium of transfer to another organism.

Another technique of genetic engineering is known as cloning. This involves the proliferation of a specific organism or one of its parts. It is also referred to as cell or tissue culture. A third technique of genetic engineering uses monoclonal antibodies, in which specific genes are manipulated to produce antibodies relevant to specific antigens. Current work in cancer therapy and diabetes research is based on this technique.

The above techniques have been used to do some amazing things in the fields of agriculture, medicine, chemistry, energy, and others. Orange juice, cocoa, vanilla, indigo, cotton fibers, and sugar-replacing sweeteners have been produced by cloning, for example. Since 1981 more than 100 different foreign genes, including human and virus genes, have been spliced into laboratory mice. One experiment produced mice twice normal size. Foreign genes have been transferred to pigs, sheep, and fish.

Genetically engineered insulin and interferon are already on the market, as is a vaccine for hepatitis B. Some 5,000 children afflicted with human growth deficiency are using a genetically engineered human-growth hormone to correct the disorder.

In agriculture, scientists have genetically engineered a growth hormone for milk cows, the bovine-growth hormone BGH. BGH has experimentally increased milk production in cows by 25 to 30 percent. It is ironic that while the U.S. government has been paying to buy out whole herds of dairy cows to decrease surplus milk supplies, it has also been supporting research on BGH, which may increase milk production.

While the many potential benefits of genetic engineering can be enumerated at length, the technology has escalated so rapidly that society has not been able to fully evaluate its implications. There are moral, ethical, social, and political areas of concern involved. Because the field of biotechnology is so technically complex, there is the ever-present danger that decisions regarding its control will be left only to government regulators and/or the scientists. The issues here are much too important for that to happen.

Fundamental Questions

Biotechnology involves the essence of created life, including the human dimension. Until now, new varieties (species) of plants and animals present on earth have arisen only from the created order, as far as we know. Now scientists have the capability of creating new varieties by manipulating the genetic material itself. The integrity of the created order is at stake. This is the key issue which Christians need to examine more fully.

In addition to this fundamental issue, there are other concerns about this new technology. Among them are the following:

• *The patenting of animals and plants* by those who have done the manipulation. Should animals and plants be considered patentable along with machines and gadgets? Should corporations control genetic material for profit, since it is a part of the created order? Are not living things a part of our common heritage? Who really owns them? Psalm 24:1 says, "The earth is the Lord's, and everything in it."

• *The release of genetically altered organisms* into the environment. It is uncertain how new types of organisms, especially microorganisms, will adapt when introduced into the existing environment. There is the possibility that some such introductions may bring havoc to the present ecosystem. Who should decide if and when such an organism should be released?

• *Side effects of genetic engineering.* When nuclear energy was discovered, some scientists claimed that electricity from its application would be so cheap that it would "not even have to be metered." By now we know there are serious side effects from nuclear technology, and it is costly in many ways. The laws of nature indicate that there will be side effects from genetic engineering, some of which may be catastrophic. There is no free (or cheap) lunch in nature. The benefits from genetic engineering will most certainly result in costs, observable or hidden.

• *The control of biotechnology.* Recent developments in the industrialized world raise questions about the control of biotechnology for financial profit. Since April 1987 animal patenting has been permitted, and plants have been patented for more than 10 years. Public universities receive funds from corporations for biotechnical research, but then these corporations gain control of

the product or processes. Multinational corporations have en-
larged and restructured greatly in recent years around biotechnology. Today it is common to find chemical, pharmaceutical,
energy, and agribusiness companies all combined into one massive multinational corporation. With these developments there is
a question about who will benefit the most from "advances" in
genetic engineering. Is regulation possible that would assure both
the public good and ecojustice (economic and economic equity;
see chapter 4, above)?

Earthkeepers' Questions

Further questions in need of study include: What is responsible
technology? Can it be neutral? How does today's technology affect the created world? Affect poor people? What are the most appropriate ways to assist today's hungry within the constraints of
nature's (God's) laws? Is the present worldview that science and
technology can solve any human problems compatible with the
Christian worldview? If not, what should be done about it? With
the Nuclear Age already here and now the arrival of the Age of Biotechnology, the Christian church faces serious discussion on its
urgent agenda.

These and other questions about biotechnology must be faced
if we are to help shape an equitable and sustainable society. As
part of its mandate to tend the creation, the church must be involved in this shaping.

Cal DeWitt, environmental ethics professor at the University of
Wisconsin, suggests that "the Lord's earth has become seriously
degraded environmentally because of human arrogance, ignorance and greed."

These same human characteristics are involved in the field of
biotechnology today, as are more noble motivations and scientific
zeal. Might the results of this new technology contribute further
to the environmental sickness of the Lord's earth? It behooves all
of us who claim to be stewards of God's good creation to find out
—and to act appropriately.

Discussion Questions

1. In what respects is genetic engineering similar to traditional plant and animal husbandry? How is it different?

2. What evidence is there that genetic engineering is perceived to be an important field in science and agriculture today?

3. Define genetic engineering in the simplest terms possible.

4. Interpret this statement by Rifkin: "The great underlying myth of the Biotechnical Revolution is that it is possible to accelerate the production of more efficient living utilities without ever running out."

5. In what sense can the age of genetic engineering be considered a second green revolution?

6. Why is loss of wild-type genes in plant crops a serious issue?

7. Discuss the pros and cons of plant and animal patenting.

8. How can biotechnology be considered a double-edged sword for the Third World?

9. The statement that "there is no free lunch in nature" is made in connection with genetic engineering. Explain.

10. What is the role of wild genes in agricultural production?

11. What is threatening species and wild-gene loss? How can it be stopped?

12. Answer the committee's questions near the beginning of chapter 30, on animal patenting.

13. Do you agree that "the integrity of the created order is at stake" with the proliferation of biotechnology? Why or why not?

14. Who should control genetic engineering, or shouldn't it be controlled? What is the role of the church on the subject?

Resources

Berardi, Gigi M., ed. *World Food, Population, and Development.* Rowman and Allansheld, 1986. Chapter 28: "Biotechnology, Seeds, and the Restructuring of Agriculture."

Doyle, Jack. *Altered Harvest: Agricultural Genetics and the Fate of the World's Food Supply.* New York: Viking Press, 1985.

Fragile Harvest, The. A 50-minute VHS video cassette. National

Film Board of Canada. Pros and cons of biotechnology. Available for free loan from MCC, Akron, PA 17501; or MCC Manitoba, 134 Plaza Drive, Winnipeg, MB R3T 5K9.

Multinational Monitor. Entire 28 February 1986 issue of this periodical is devoted to genetic engineering: *Genetic Roulette*. For back copy, contact *Multinational Monitor*, 1346 Connecticut Ave., N.W., Room 411, Washington, DC 20036.

Rifkin, Jeremy. *Declaration of a Heretic*. Boston: Routledge and Kegan Hall, 1985. Rifkin is a critic of nuclear technology and genetic engineering. He clearly states why in this book.

Energy and Environment

The earth dries up and withers,
the world languishes and withers,
the exalted of the earth languish.
        —Isaiah 24:4

Do not store up for yourselves treasures on earth,
    where moth and rust destroy,
    and where thieves break in and steal.
But store up for yourselves treasures in heaven.
        —Matthew 6:19-20a

The sun and the moon and the stars would have disappeared long
ago . . . had they happened to be within the reach of predatory
human hands.
        —Havelock Ellis, quoted in *Beyond Oil*

32. Panic in the Persian Gulf: World Oil Crisis

The eyes of the industrialized world are focused on the Persian Gulf whenever there are signals that the precious oil supply from the region is in danger of being disrupted. The modern world would become hopelessly paralyzed were that Gulf oil to cease flowing. A brief look at facts and statistics on world oil production, consumption, and reserves will reveal why there is such concern by the industrial countries of the world to keep the Gulf open.

Cheap Oil Today

Cheap energy is what makes the affluent lifestyle of the industrialized world possible. That's what oil provides. Industry, agriculture, and transportation—as well as the military machine—are precariously dependent upon immense amounts of oil. The most recent data show that 42.8 percent of the energy consumed by industrial nations is in the form of oil (*British Petroleum Statistical Review of World Energy 1987*).

Oil is in finite supply. It is running out. About that there is no debate. "By 1986 nearly half of all oil discovered had already been consumed. . . . *In North America four-fifths of all the oil discovered to date has already been burned.* Current proven reserves total 36 billion barrels, enough to supply U.S. needs for less than eight years at current rates of use" (*State of the World 1987*, page 11, with emphasis added).

Data from the U.S. National Information Center (May 1986) is even more pessimistic. According to NIC, the United States used almost six billion barrels of oil in 1985. U.S. oil reserves total only 28 billion barrels, they report. If only domestic oil were used at that rate, it would last less than five years.

Canadian oil reserves (known) total over 445 million barrels. If Canada relied only on domestic production of readily accessible conventional oil, there would be only about 10 years known reserve left. If Arctic and offshore oil is included, Canada's supply would last about 15 years. Domestic oil alone will not be used by Canada and the U.S. They will simply import oil as needed.

As of 1987, Canada was importing about 35 percent, while the U.S. was importing about 40 percent of its oil. Conservation and world recession combined to reduce oil imports somewhat from 1979 highs.

According to *World Resources 1987*, however, U.S. oil demand in the first six months of 1986 rose 2.1 percent from that same period in 1985. This was due to an improved economy, a new speed limit of 65 miles per hour for cars on some interstates, and General Motors and Ford convincing the government to lower fuel efficiency standards from 27.5 to 26 miles/gallon for cars sold after 1985. One can assume that oil use in the U.S. will increase in the next few years. This will bring more pressure for increased oil imports, which rose to about 50 percent of U.S. consumption by 1990, when Iraq occupied Kuwait and there was worldwide alarm.

To reduce dependence on imported oil from OPEC (Organization of Petroleum Exporting Countries), the U.S. has increased domestic production and imported from other countries. Data from *World Resources 1987* reveals surprising changes in oil production from 1980 to 1985. The Middle East, with vast reserves of oil, reduced production by 42.6 percent during that time, while Western Europe increased its production by 57.5 percent.

The distribution of the world's remaining oil reserves is more unbalanced now than ever. Ninety-five percent of the world's proven oil reserves are in 20 countries. Arab nations and Iran control 56.3 percent of the world's total. Most petroleum reserves will become increasingly concentrated in the Middle East as Arab states and Iran cut their production and non-OPEC countries rapidly pump out their oil.

The news about finding more oil reserves is not encouraging. For example, the book *Beyond Oil* states: "More oil discoveries in the lower 48 states are highly unlikely because there is not enough room between existing holes to contain them. As of 1975 there was one production or exploratory well for every 1.6 square kilometers of sedimentary rock, the only kind known to contain oil in the continental U.S." (page 58). This is not to say that there will be no new discoveries of oil. There will be some. But discoveries will not keep up with the exhaustion of existing reserves. That is a consensus of oil geologists today.

It is easy to see why the Middle East with only 4 percent of the world's people but 56 percent of the world's oil reserves is such a strategic region in today's world. North America has about 5 percent of the world's people but only 6 percent of the oil reserves. Yet in 1985 there was more oil pumped out of North America (578.5 million metric tons) than was pumped out of the Middle East (532.5 million metric tons), according to *World Resources 1987* (page 97).

Oil Addicts

It is clear that the U.S. and other non-Arab nations are rapidly using up their remaining oil. The Indian subcontinent has about one billion people (20 percent of the global population) but less than 1 percent of the world's oil reserves. China also has a billion people—and less than 3 percent of the world's oil reserves. Japan has no oil reserves at all. Europe is pumping down its oil reserves at a rapid rate. Russia also is looking beyond its considerable reserves to the Middle East.

The industrialized world is hooked on petroleum. When oil was "discovered" and first pumped at Titusville, Pennsylvania, in 1859, world population was about one billion. Energy needs were modest. Today, world population is over five billion. Modern agriculture, industry, and transportation will be hard pressed to support this large population by current methods with a dwindling supply of oil. The difficulty of providing sufficient energy for the world's vast and growing population has not been recognized.

Unfortunately, a temporary oversupply of oil occurred in the Western world during the 1980s because of a worldwide recession and conservation measures. People no longer believe the oil supply is limited. The U.S. administration and Congress have removed incentives for conservation practices. Business as usual has been espoused. The day of reckoning has been postponed, made more ominous but not removed.

Earthkeepers' Response

Only as the links between geography and oil use are recognized and accepted by all governments and individuals, will solutions to the Persian Gulf tensions be found. The industrialized world can be weaned from oil dependency. It will not be easy. There is a large supply of coal in North America, and less polluting ways to use it are being developed. But the true costs of reclaiming surface-mined land are high. Nuclear energy has not fulfilled its earlier promise because of problems of contaminating the earth.

The long-term answer lies in commitment to an environmentally responsible lifestyle—use of renewable energy sources such as the sun, wind, hydro, biomass, and other conservation practices. These are activities in which Christians can take the lead, individually and corporately. Conservation and using renewable energy will help protect the global environment, God's good earth.

33. Agriculture, Food Systems, and the Energy Crisis

There is an ongoing farm economic crisis in North America. The severity of the problem was masked by substantial government subsidies during the late 1980s. This was due in part to the cost of energy needed for production. Food prices to the farmer have not kept up with increases in the cost of petroleum and such derivatives as fertilizer, herbicides, and pesticides.

To deal with a cost-price squeeze, some U.S. farmers have historically expanded production acreage. They farmed "fence row to fence row," plowing up marginal land, and paying little attention to soil conservation practices.

Cheap Food Policy

U.S. consumers have for decades enjoyed a cheap-food policy which discounted the hidden cost of exploiting the soil and the fossil fuel supply. They have become accustomed to paying an average of only 17 to 18 percent of their income for food. Increasing food prices are politically volatile, and farmers are rarely organized to act in concert. Processing companies usually dictate prices paid to farmers, and food producers are unable to pass on increasing costs of production.

The following data from *The World Almanac 1984* illustrate how food prices paid to farmers have dramatically lagged behind increasing wages between 1950 and 1982. The average hourly wage for a factory worker in 1950 was about $1.65. In 1982, it was $8.50, more than five times that amount. Prices paid to farmers increased by much less, as true even to the present.

Food Prices Paid To Farmers (Averages)

Product	1950	1982	Factor Increase
Average Factory Wage	$1.65/hr.	$8.50/hr.	5.2
Chicken (Broilers)	$0.274/lb.	$0.269/lb.	0.0
Corn	$2.00/bu.	$2.65/bu.	1.3
Eggs	$0.363/dz.	$0.595/dz.	1.6
Oats	$0.79/bu.	$1.45/bu.	1.8
Cattle (Beef)	$23.30/cwt.	$56.70/cwt.	2.2
Wheat	$1.52/bu.	$3.53/bu.	2.3
Hogs	$18.00/cwt.	$52.30/cwt.	2.8
Milk	$3.89/cwt.	$13.60/cwt.	3.4

According to the 1984 *Fact Book of U.S. Agriculture*, the average hourly pay of a typical factory worker in 1950 could purchase 10.1 pounds of bread, 2.5 pounds of chicken, 8 quarts of milk, or 2.4 dozen eggs. By 1982 that same worker could buy 16.3 pounds of bread, 11.9 pounds of chicken, 15.2 quarts of milk or 9.8 dozen eggs.

To accommodate this cheap-food policy in the U.S. a capital-intensive form of agriculture that is environmentally degrading has developed. Energy use has increased dramatically. Fertilizer derived from oil and natural gas is being consumed at 15 times the 1930 rate. Tractor power is 11 times the 1930 rate and tractors number 5.1 times the 1930 level.

Seventeen percent of all fossil-fuel energy used in the U.S. goes into the food-production system for growing, processing, and distribution, according to professor David Pimentel of Cornell University.

It is important to note that in 1983 about 72 percent of food costs to consumers was to move the food from farm to table. This involved assembling, inspecting, grading, storing, processing, wholesaling, and retailing. Only 28 percent of the consumer food dollar went to the farm producer.

Huge Energy Input

Large amounts of energy are required in our food and agricultural system today. Sorrells and Pimentel illustrate this dramatically in an article, "Food Energy and the Environment," in the *American Biology Teacher* (April 1981). They show that a 2.2 pound can of sweet corn which has 825 calories of food energy requires 6,560 calories of energy to put on the table. The energy involved is itemized like this: home preparation, 1,005 calories; shopping, 680 calories; distribution, 750 calories; transport, 350 calories; factory canning, 2,210 calories; processing, 575 calories; and growing, 990 calories.

It is curious to note that only 15 percent of the total energy input comes from growing the corn (990 calories). Transportation of food in the U.S. is also energy expensive. A head of lettuce contains about 50 calories of food energy; just to move it by truck from California to New York requires 1,800 calories. To fly 2.2 pounds of strawberries (354 calories of food energy) from California to New York takes 30,700 calories. Overall, most sources claim that in U.S. agriculture it takes about 10 calories of energy input to put one calorie of food on the table. Eight of those calories are for transportation and two for production.

The use of energy in our food system has increased faster than energy use in any other sector. Large quantities of fuel are used in making fertilizers, pesticides, and machinery for farms and for food transportation. Additional fuel is used to operate the machinery, for irrigation, and for other farm processes.

Furthermore, fossil fuel-intensive agricultural practices add to environmental pollution and contribute to serious degradation of land and water resources. Soil erosion has already caused significant losses of cropland and reductions in agricultural productivity in the U.S. and elsewhere.

In light of known fossil-fuel limitations, we can no longer afford to waste energy and degrade land, water, and air resources in order to produce food. A new energy crisis will mandate that we modify our present food-system practices and develop alternative methods to meet the increasing need for food in the world.

Earthkeepers' Response

The Sorrells-Pimentel article contains recommendations for accomplishing an alternate food system and a more sustainable type of agriculture. They believe at least 50 percent of the fossil energy now used could be saved while maintaining crop yields and improving environmental quality. Among their recommendations:

- Reduce animal protein consumption by half and increase quantities of grains, legumes, and other vegetables consumed by the population.
- Decrease the number of individually packaged foods and encourage the use of recyclable containers.
- Select livestock and crops based on nutrient content and energy efficiency of production.
- Whenever possible, locate food-production facilities close to consumer markets.
- Use farm machinery appropriate to the task and acreage cultivated.
- Increase the use of livestock and green manures.
- Employ nonchemical biological and cultural pest controls instead of pesticides where possible.
- Control soil erosion and water runoff by using crop rotation, contour planting, terracing, cover crops, and leaving crop remains on the surface of the land.
- Initiate land-use policies ensuring sufficient arable land for cultivation to meet the future needs of the nation.
- Increase crop production in areas that receive sufficient natural rainfall; when irrigation is necessary, use water and energy wisely.

There are many small groups working toward an agriculture that is energy efficient, ecologically and environmentally sound, and sustainable. Among these are the Land Institute at Salina, Kansas; Rodale Farms near Kutztown, Pennsylvania; and the Center for Rural Affairs at Walthill, Nebraska. More and more farmers are turning to a less capital-intensive farming system. MCC (Mennonite Central Committee) agriculturists in the Third World practice this kind of farming.

Are we morally justified to participate in a food and agricultural system that exploits our nonrenewable natural resources and degrades the environment? If not, how can the present unsustainable food system be changed in view of future world needs? Who is going to initiate that change and when? What roles does the church have in these issues?

What is needed at this time is a food and agricultural system that is at the same time ecologically and economically sustainable. For this to occur, Christians must be enthusiastic advocates for the difficult changes that farmers will have to make in the future.

Discussion Questions

1. Review reasons given for the oil glut during the middle and late 1980s. Which reasons seem most plausible? Least?

2. How long do you think a good supply of oil will be available to North America? On what do you base your judgment?

3. Why has the North American populace been using more oil since the 1979 shortage? Do you think the oil supply should be conserved? Why, or why not?

4. Why was more oil pumped out of the ground in the U.S. in 1985 than in the Middle East, even though nearly 60 percent of the remaining oil on earth is there?

5. Compare the population and oil reserves of the Middle East with those of the U.S. Reflect on the "panic."

6. How is cheap American food related to the oil supply?

7. Analyze the recommendations for a sustainable food system listed in chapter 33. Which do you think are most feasible? Which are more workable as truer energy or environmental costs are included in what the consumer pays?

8. What role does the church have to play in resolving the issues described in these articles? What is a just, sustainable farm and food-production policy?

Resources

Flavin, Christopher. *World Oil: Coping with the Dangers of Success.*
    Worldwatch Paper 66. Worldwatch Institute, 1776 Mass. Ave.
    NW, Washington, DC 20036.

Grever, John, and others. *Beyond Oil: The Threat to Food and Fuel in the Coming Decades*. Cambridge, Mass.: Ballinger Publishing Co., 1986, for Carrying Capacity, Inc. An excellent, basic, easy-to-understand description of the issues, by the Complex Systems Research Center of the University of New Hampshire.

State of the World 1986, State of the World 1987, and *State of the World 1988*. Worldwatch Institute. Good discussions on oil.

World Resources 1987 and *World Resources 1988-89*. Good data on oil. World Resources Institute, 1709 New York Ave. NW, Washington, DC 20006.

PART FIVE

Sustainable Agriculture

Sustainable Society

Behold, I will create new heavens and a new earth.
The former things will not be remembered. . . .
They will build houses and dwell in them;
  they will plant vineyards and eat their fruit.
They will not toil in vain
  or bear children doomed to misfortune;
for they will be a people blessed by the Lord. . . .
The wolf and the lamb will feed together,
and the lion will eat straw like the ox. . . .
They will neither harm nor destroy
  in all my holy mountain.
      —Isaiah 65:17, 21, 23, 25

We have not inherited the earth from our fathers,
we are borrowing it from our children.
      —Lester R. Brown, in *Building a Sustainable Society*

34. What Is a Sustainable Society?

We sometimes refer to the ideal society as one that is just, participatory, and sustainable. In this chapter we will examine what is meant by a sustainable society.

All living things, including people, are wholly dependent upon natural resources and energy for their physical existence. Planet earth is a vast, balanced natural system in which physical materials are continually being recycled. Water, oxygen, carbon, nitrogen, phosphorous, and other vital substances are recycled between the nonliving environment and the living world with systematic regularity.

But energy, so critical in sustaining life, is not recyclable. It travels an amazing one-way street from the sun through green plants to other organisms. The amount of life is limited primarily by the amount of energy that green plants can incorporate into food, although space, pollution, disease, and other natural factors also limit the number of organisms.

Recognizing Limits

The number of living things in a certain location at a specific time is called a population. Population size and density are affected by four factors: birth rate, death rate, immigration, and emigration. These four factors interact with the availability of natural resources and energy to produce a population that functions over time in natural balance—one that is sustainable.

However, the current rate of growth of the human world population is not sustainable. Two events have allowed the human population to increase drastically:

• Humans have obtained more food by greatly increasing the immediately available energy supply, tapping enormous amounts of nonrenewable fossil fuels—petroleum, natural gas, and coal.

• Improved methods in medicine have reduced the death rate.

In 1987 the world's population reached five billion. By 1998, only 11 years later, it will be six billion, according to projections.

Clearly the human population cannot grow like this indefinitely. Society as it is now developing is not sustainable. We are dependent on a dwindling supply of fossil fuels. We are exploiting many other natural resources needed to sustain and maintain the world's population—present and future.

We cannot morally continue depleting energy and resources at the present rate in the short term, knowing such consumption is physically impossible in the long term. Christians must make some changes if they believe that "the earth is the Lord's and all that is in it, the world, and those who live in it" (Psalm 24:1, NRSV).

Our economic systems generally do not recognize the laws of nature regarding environmental sustainability. Continued population growth and economic expansion will put more and more stress on natural ecosystems.

Lester R. Brown says:

> Supply side economics with its overriding emphasis on production and its nearly blind faith in market forces will lead to serious problems. . . . The market has no alarm that sounds when the carrying capacity of a biological system is exceeded. . . . In a world where the population has passed the four billion mark and is nearing five billion, the unalloyed working of the market forces can destroy the very croplands, forests, grasslands and fisheries that support the economy. (Worldwatch Paper 48).

Earthkeepers' Response

What can or should be done to solve the population imbalance and the depletion of natural resources? How can responsible Christians work toward a society that is sustainable?

Brown suggests six steps to a sustainable society: stabilizing world population, protecting cropland, reforesting the earth, moving beyond the throwaway society, conserving energy, and developing renewable energy.

35. Recycling and the Environment

*The rich forests and farmlands will be totally destroyed,
 in the same way that a fatal sickness destroys a man.
There will be so few trees left
 that even a child will be able to count them.*
            —Isaiah 10:18-19 (TEV)

The prophet Isaiah, before the birth of Christ, described the exploitation of the environment as a disease. Using the earth's resources unwisely is a problem that seems to have been present in the world from earliest times.

Scrap Drives

One of my, Jocele's, earliest recollections of an organized effort to use resources wisely centers in the collection and recycling of paper during the 1940s. I recall how our family saved paper for the school and community "scrap" drives. We must have decided that this was a permissible activity for peace-minded people during those war years.

Today, for ecological as well as economic reasons, it is essential that recycling efforts be redoubled and carried out in an organized way.

Why has a sudden, concerted emphasis developed on recycling? The barge of New York City garbage that was without a home for weeks in summer 1987 called public attention to the fact that it is becoming increasingly more difficult to find an "away" for used items. Many community landfill sites are filled to the brim and overflowing. Land in highly populated areas is already at a premium for housing and local needs. Businesses must find safe ways to dispose of industrial wastes, many of them toxic.

Continued studies and news reports indicate that recycling is bigger than saving paper at home and selling it to the local scrap dealer. Local and national governments and private businesses are involved in the recycling industry, dealing with glass, paper, metal products, and a variety of other materials.

Recycling

Recycling is using wastes instead of virgin materials in making new products. It can be remaking the original product from the wastes (reclaiming lead from old car batteries to make new) or the use of wastes in a different product (shredding newspapers for cellulose insulation).

Recycling accomplishes several purposes:
- It conserves virgin materials.
- It protects the environment by easing pressure on undeveloped wild areas.
- It reduces the cost of waste disposal and the need to devote so much more land to dumps.
- It saves energy in the manufacturing process.
- Since raw materials are usually imported, recycling promotes local economic development.

Use of raw materials from developing countries by industrially developed countries frequently means that workers and the land in those countries have been exploited by adverse conditions and policies. They have been reduced to economic bondage as "hewers of wood and drawers of water" (Joshua 9:21, KJV).

With increasing amounts of waste and fewer landfill sites, costs of disposal have risen sharply. An article in *The Christian Science Monitor* (10 July 1987) states that in St. Paul, Minnesota, costs for recycling a ton of waste through recycling were $30. But landfill costs per ton were $90 and rising, and incineration costs were $90-110 for the same ton. All other concerns aside, it is economically advantageous to consider recycling as a viable option.

Wealthy Wastrels

It is evident by comparison with lifestyles a generation or two ago that the richer we are the more we waste. The increased number of two-income families has also altered lifestyles, contributing to today's throwaway society.

The *Monitor* article proposed that all the energy consumed in the world each year at the turn of the century be represented by a single phonograph record. Then today's annual energy consumption would require a stack of records considerably higher than the Empire State Building. Recycling can play a major role in controlling the world's energy appetite.

Most consumer goods today are destined for a one-night stand, exacerbating the waste disposal problem. They are purchased, consumed, and discarded with little regard for their remaining value. This attitude is so deeply rooted in public thinking that proposals to shift from one disposal site to another or from landfill to waste-to-energy plants are thought to be radical.

Recycling offers communities the opportunity to trim their waste disposal needs, thereby reducing disposal costs. It also eases environmental stresses. It is an effective way to slow the buildup of greenhouse gases and scale back the pollutants that contribute to acid rain.

In industrial countries, packaging contributes about 30 percent of the weight and 50 percent of the volume of household waste. Food and yard wastes account for most of the remainder. The average American discards almost 300 kilograms (about 660 pounds) of packaging each year (Worldwatch Paper 76).

Conservation Through Recycling

The following figures from a Worldwatch study list energy savings realized from recycling. The numbers indicate the percent of energy required for products made from recycled material as compared to producing from original source.

Aluminum	6	Paper	20-40
Copper	10	Glass	92
Iron and steel	35		

Recycled newsprint reduces pressure on forests since a ton of recycled newsprint saves a ton of wood, equal to about a dozen trees. Cynthia Pollock, Worldwatch Institute, says, "Simply recovering the print run of a Sunday issue of *The New York Times* would leave 75,000 trees standing."

Recycling efforts in nine of the world's 11 largest paper-consuming nations spared more than 400,000 hectares of trees in 1984. It simultaneously conserved water and energy and reduced the amount of air and water pollution that otherwise would have occurred (Worldwatch Paper 76).

Recycling rates for commonly used materials such as aluminum, paper, and glass are on the upswing in many industrial countries. The paper recovery rate seems to have reached a plateau worldwide. Japan and the Netherlands collect more than half their aluminum, paper, and glass for recycling. They require no raw materials for making their paper and glass one year out of two (Worldwatch Paper 76).

The total amount of aluminum recovered in 1985 by 10 selected industrial countries eliminated the need for five large power plants. When plastics are recycled, twice as much energy is saved as is produced by burning them in an incinerator to generate power (Worldwatch Paper 76). The advent of degradable plastics may change this picture somewhat.

Since 1981, more than half the 300 billion aluminum cans sold have been returned for recycling. The average can that comes from a store is remelted and back on supermarket shelves within six weeks. Largely because of stepped-up recycling programs, the industry used 22 percent less energy to produce a pound of aluminum in 1984 than in 1972.

Waste volumes will not be reduced significantly until products, packages, and materials are designed for durability, reuse, and recycling. A uniform national policy to standardize packaging and containers would have a far-reaching effect in decreasing materials used and in simplifying recycling. For example, Denmark is considering a system of standard bottle sizes. Bottlers could draw on a common inventory, changing only the labels. Transporting and storing these standardized containers would be greatly simplified. I recall the universal "rum bottle" used in Grenada for most locally bottled products, including honey, cooking oil, and milk.

A global transition to less dependence on recycled materials has begun. Higher energy and materials prices, emerging environmental problems, and the development of new technologies are pushing toward this transformation. Engineering techniques and materials needed to design superdurable goods are at hand. In a sustainable society, durability and recycling will replace planned obsolescence as the economy's organizing principle. Then virgin materials will be seen not as a primary source of materials but as a supplement to the existing stock.

Earthkeepers' Response

Anyone can begin recycling:

- Locate a recycling center by checking the yellow pages and newspaper ads.
- Cooperate with neighborhood and community groups that promote recycling.
- Encourage local government to recycle rather than dump.
- Reserve convenient space in your house or garage for containers for newspaper, garden compost, glass, recyclable metal (aluminum and tin), recyclable plastic, and nonrecyclables (some plastics and waxed cartons). Regularly empty these. Items accepted for recycling vary according to community and market. Household plastics are recycled in some areas. They are shredded and used in upholstered furniture, or experimentally made into waterproof construction materials for waterfront docks.
- Purchase products in containers that can be reused or

recycled. Avoid throwaways when possible. Choose paper over plastic.

- Carry your own shopping bag on shopping trips.
- Promote returnable bottle legislation.

A Sunday school class in Ohio was motivated to sponsor a community recycling project after studying some of the current world problems. This is their way of promoting more responsible living. Group support lightens the load of preparing materials for pickup and lessens discouragement in the project.

A group in Ohio has built a small neighborhood shelter with separate containers for various recyclables. Residents are encouraged to place glass, paper, and aluminum cans here. When containers are full, they are taken to the local recycling center. In this rural community, food and plant refuse are turned into compost for gardens. This is a gesture to respond as individuals to the waste problem as well and to use resources responsibly.

States with bottle laws to require recycling cans and bottles, seem to have fewer problems with littering. At a church camp in Michigan, a state with a bottle law, cans were bagged to be returned. Dealers were paying 10 cents for each can returned.

At the individual level, recycling gives us the chance to help exercise control over at least one part of our complex larger economy. By reducing the amount of waste they produce and recycling a large share of their discards, individuals can become a part of the solution.

Consumers, however, cannot effect widespread changes on their own. They need assistance from industries willing to manufacture recyclable products and governments willing to alter their waste management practices. Recycling industries will operate if there are adequate ways to make use of the finished products. Individuals can encourage businesses, schools, and governments to use recycled materials such as paper. Consumers must ask for items made from recycled materials and in some cases pay more for them.

Individually we must remember to practice "living simply so that others may simply live." This requires a responsible lifestyle that thoughtfully cherishes creation, including all parts of the environment and its inhabitants. Unless current practices are changed, we are literally throwing away our future.

"With our heritage of frugality and thrift, we Mennonites should be pioneers in reprocessing. It's extra work to collect or store items for recycling and much easier to throw away, but are we looking for the easy way?" (*Living More with Less*).

Discussion Questions

1. How does the cycling of physical materials in earth's systems differ from the cycling of energy? How does this relate to sustainability?

2. Review the factors that determine population size and density.

3. Discuss the two events mentioned that have combined to produce a human population explosion on earth today.

4. Ponder the steps needed (as suggested by Lester R. Brown) for moving toward a sustainable society. How does each relate to a sustainable society?

5. Evaluate the positive consequences of recycling as mentioned in that article. Explain each.

6. Why is there such a concerted emphasis on recycling in North America today?

7. Examine the suggestions given for individual responses to recycling. React to them. Are there others you think of?

8. Relate recycling to a sustainable society. How important is it? Is it an option or a necessity? How does it relate to the poor? To justice?

Resources

Brown, Lester R. *Building a Sustainable Society*. New York: W. W. Norton Co., 1981. Classic treatment, from Worldwatch Institute, 1776 Mass. Ave. NW, Washington, DC 20036.

Brown, Lester R., and Pamela Shaw. *Six Steps to a Sustainable Society*. Worldwatch Paper 48. Worldwatch Institute.

Heloise. *Hints for a Healthy Planet*. New York: Putnam, 1990. On reusing, recycling, and resourcefulness.

Longacre, Doris J. *Living More with Less*. Scottdale, Pa.: Herald Press, 1980.

Pollock, Cynthia. *Mining Urban Wastes: The Potential for Recycling.*
   Worldwatch Paper 76, April 1987. Worldwatch Institute.
Void of Desolation, A. Friendship Press, 1985. A 16-minute
   filmstrip. Free loan from MCC, Akron, PA 17501.

The Family Farm

The earth is the Lord's, and everything in it,
  the world, and all who live in it.
    —Psalm 24:1

The Lord God took the man
  and put him in the Garden of Eden
  to work it and take care of it.
    —Genesis 2:15

Family farming brings with it certain democratic and community
values—widespread ownership of economic resources, equality of
opportunity, a belief in the dignity of work and the integrity of the
individual, and a concern for the good of the community.
    —Marty Strange, in *Hope for the Family Farm*

36. Ways to Resolve the North American Farm Crisis

The North American farm crisis is continuing. Every year thousands of farmers are forced out of business. Other sectors of the food industry thrive. U.S. consumers spend less than 18 percent of their disposable income on food. Economic prosperity for the employed nonfarm majority abounds. What can be done to assure that farmers will receive a more equitable return on their food production?

In one recent year, the U.S. Department of Agriculture (USDA) listed per capita food expenditures as $1,738. Disposable income for the same year averaged $9,892 per capita. This means that only 17.6 percent of per capita income went for food in the U.S. Most people in the world spend upwards of 50 percent of their income for food. Many Americans could spend more for food without undue sacrifice.

Food processors and other middlemen take far more than their fair share of the food dollar. During a recent Christmas holiday, we were made aware of a curious paradox—farm prices for grain commodities had been decreasing that year, but processed cereal prices were increasing. We did a few calculations that astounded us after buying some Corn Chex and Wheat Chex for our traditional homemade snack mix.

Corn Chex cost $1.90 for a 17.5-ounce box ($1.82 per pound).

Corn was bringing $2.22 per bushel on the market. Since a bushel of shelled corn weighs about 56 pounds, the cost per pound is about 4 cents. At this rate, a $2.22 bushel of corn should make over $102 worth of Corn Chex. We realize that there are costs for processing, distributing, advertising, and retailing, but how can those costs be so incredibly high?

About the same time we were able to purchase locally ground cornmeal at a farm market for only 20 cents per pound. This is a good reason for buying locally grown, minimally handled food, and it illustrates again the intolerably high processed-food markup.

The calculations for Wheat Chex were similar. A box costs $2.15 for 22 ounces ($1.55 per pound). Wheat was selling for $3.03 per bushel. For a 60-pound bushel the producer received about 5 cents per pound. At that rate about $93 worth of Wheat Chex could be produced from a $3.03 bushel of wheat. Again, processing costs seem out of line. We wrote to the processing company to ask about their processing and advertising costs. They told us that those were "industry secrets."

Adequate Compensation for Farmers

It is obvious that the farmer is generally not realizing an adequate return on produce. The cheap-food policy promoted (and controlled) by our present political-economic system, and demanded by urban consumers, encourages farmers to farm more "efficiently." This means farmers have economic incentive to produce commodities for the lowest unit cost possible. True environmental costs to natural resources used in production do not show up in dollars and cents. However, in terms of soil erosion, chemical pollution, use of nonrenewable fossil fuels, and the demise of the family farm, the cheap-food policy actually results in expensive food.

Consumers can reduce their food costs and return more to the producer by purchasing locally grown foods and those requiring less processing. This is one way to counter some of the negative costs referred to before.

On a broader scale, food processors, grain merchants, and

handlers in our food systems must be better monitored and regulated to counter profiteering. Vertical integration (corporate control of a commodity from producer to consumer) of food corporations must be better regulated for the same reason. This will take popular support for strong governmental action.

Another way to give farmers adequate compensation is through appropriate government-commodity price supports. This has been done for some time. Critics of present support systems charge that many farmers who really need help are not receiving it. On the other hand, one large cotton farm in California received more than $20 million in government subsidies in 1986.

One suggestion is that government-commodity price supports be given only to those farmers who will practice a sustainable type of agriculture. The USDA has made soil-conservation farm plans mandatory for farmers to receive benefits after 1990. Incentives could also be given for approved water-conservation practices and energy efficiency. Disincentives could be devised to discourage practices that lead to environmental degradation.

Another way to work at the problem of inadequate return to the producer would be to place a surcharge (a tax) on the food purchased by consumers and return that money to farms in the form of targeted subsidies as described above.

As an example, suppose the surcharge on food were sufficient to raise the percentage of personal disposable income spent for food in the U.S. from 18 percent to 23 percent. Alongside most people in the world spending over 50 percent of their income for food, this is a modest 5-percent increase. Using the USDA figures quoted earlier, it averages about $458 per capita.

Multiplying $458 by the U.S. population (240 million) would result in about $110 billion annually. If this money were made available to the 2.2 million present U.S. family farms, each one would receive an average $50,000 more annual income. That would be enough to save many imperiled farms.

If the $458-per-person food surcharge seems excessive, it should be compared with the per capita expenditure for the U.S. military—$1,254 in 1986.

How does a $110 billion subsidy as calculated above compare with recent government agricultural subsidies? In 1985, the total subsidy paid out to U.S. farmers was about $18 billion (only $75 per citizen). In 1986 it was about $26 billion ($108 per capita). Compared with other federal expenditures, farm subsidies are not as excessive as many believe. It has been difficult, however, to appropriately target those subsidies to the farmers in need.

Earthkeepers' Response

Compensating family farmers who practice a sustainable type of agriculture equitably and adequately is complicated, but certainly possible. In today's global economy, it cannot be left entirely to the free-market system. If it is, the crisis in agriculture will continue to escalate. More family farms will be lost, erosion will increase, and environmental degradation will continue.

37. Pentagon Tax Increases Agricultural Crisis

A 1986 study showed that the U.S. military budget received $12 billion more from the nation's major agricultural counties than the federal government returned in the form of military contracts and farm program payments combined.

The study was called "Plowing Under the Farmers—The Impact of the Pentagon Tax on American Agriculture." It was done by James Anderson of Michigan State University for Employment Research Associates, a Lansing, Michigan, nonprofit organization that studies the impact of military spending on the economy. Anderson used government figures from the Pentagon, the U.S. Department of Agriculture (USDA), and the nongovernmental Tax Foundation.

The basic goal of the study was to compare the net impact of the Pentagon tax burden and expenditures with the net impact of the agricultural tax burden and expenditures. This was done in 25 states and 1,200 major agricultural counties

The 25 states studied had a Pentagon tax burden of $163.1 billion. They received $126.8 billion in military expenditures for fiscal year 1985, a loss of $36.3 billion. After allowing for federal payments and loans to the farm sector in these states, the Pentagon tax burden created a total net drain of $31 billion in 25 principal agricultural states. This was a dramatic finding.

Of the 1,200 most agricultural counties, 800 suffered a net outflow due to Pentagon tax drains which exceeded their net agricultural payments. "The consequence of this drain," the report says, "is a massive ongoing transfer of wealth from the vital agricultural sector to the unproductive military sector." The study reported that these 1,200 agricultural counties (of about 3,000 counties nationwide) sent $41.5 billion to the Pentagon. That was $22.6 billion more than they received in military payments and $12.4 billion more than they received in military and agricultural payments combined.

Misplaced Priorities

Federal tax money is returned to the farm sector through various farm-income stabilization programs as well as conservation and research programs. Anderson states that "if these programs are eliminated or drastically reduced, the deficit position of these agricultural counties would deteriorate. The most harmful federal budget priorities would be a combination of increases in military outlays and net reductions in agricultural support and conservation programs."

In a brief description of the present farm crisis, the study notes that:

- Real farm income has been driven below the levels of the entire Great Depression era.
- The real net worth of the farm sector declined for five straight years after 1981.
- Since 1981, the return on equity for the farm sector has been negative and the national agricultural debt-to-equity ratio has risen from around 20 percent in the 1970s to almost 29 percent in 1984.

The primary reason for the drop in the worth of the average farm has been the drop in prices for farm products. Agricultural exports have declined sharply in the last five years. Farm products have been hard hit by the overpriced dollar. Anderson says that "this is yet another link in the Pentagon budget, as the combination of cutting taxes and raising the military budget was the primary cause of the deficit and thus of record high real interest rates and the high dollar."

When one looks only at the USDA and its programs in evaluating the impact of the federal budget on agriculture, one might conclude that the U.S. government is subsidizing American farmers. But this new study concludes that

> the Pentagon tax outflow far exceeds the agricultural payments inflow. When we look at the flow of tax dollars out of the farm sector and into the federal government, we will find that the farm sector is in fact subsidizing the federal government, especially the costly military programs of the Pentagon. The simple fact is this: even at current levels of involvement in the farm sector, the predominantly agricultural states and counties are being depleted by the disproportionate priority given to military spending by the federal government.

Cutback of Conservation Programs

Another concern pointed up by the study is the reduction in federal soil conservation support. "The stewardship and conservation of the soil must be the foundation for a good agricultural policy. But, for the nation as a whole, federal agricultural policies and budget priorities of the last five years show a steadily decreasing commitment to the conservation of soil," Anderson wrote. Low grain prices, as seen in recent years, discourage soil conservation efforts by individual farmers. Low prices stimulate planting of marginal lands in order to cover fixed costs.

The real budget request for the U.S. Soil Conservation Service (SCS) declined from $496.7 million in fiscal year 1980 to $267.1 million for FY 1986, a decline of 46.3 percent. In 1980 the Reagan administration set the value of soil conservation for the entire U.S. at the equivalent of one B-1 bomber in its 1986 budget!

Staff positions in the SCS have been cut too. From FY 1981 through FY 1984, 528 positions were eliminated. From 1984 through 1986 the U.S. administration proposed eliminating 6,970 more staff positions in the SCS for a total staff reduction of 7,500 positions, or 57.7 percent. Meanwhile, between 1981 and 1985 over 170,000 persons were added to the armed forces.

Anderson summarized the study by noting that current and foreseeable federal policies are depleting the U.S. agricultural sector in three ways:

> First, a significant net drain of tax dollars is occurring. Federal priorities are taking far more money from farm sector counties than is being returned, and the combination of increased military spending and reduced agricultural spending would worsen the net drain and increase the harsh stress on farm communities.

> Second, agricultural payments do not close the Pentagon tax deficit in farm sector states and counties. . . . Increases in the Pentagon budget increase the burden on the farm sector.

> Third, the Reagan Administration is pursuing an active policy of malign neglect toward soil and watershed conservation . . . the neglect of the soil may in the long run prove to be one of the most short-sighted and dangerous of current federal policies.

Earthkeepers' Response

It should be noted that Christian motivation to speak out against military spending does not come from a desire to be better off economically. It comes from a desire to live a life of shalom. As the study reviewed here shows, present government policies of military spending impact on the earth itself as well as on rural agricultural communities, degrading both. If we are to be stewards, cocreators with God and concerned about our besieged rural brothers and sisters, we must find ways to counteract the militarization occurring in North America and around the world today.

38. U.S. Food and Agriculture Policy

It is estimated that 220,000 U.S. farms went out of business from 1981 to 1986 (USDA *1987 Fact Book*). Farm-loss figures for 1987 and 1988 may be somewhat reduced when the facts are in. But the agricultural crisis is far from resolved because its causes have not been addressed. Like many other modern issues, its causes and implications are complex.

From a North American point of view, the most identifiable problem of agriculture is overproduction of food commodities. Victor Ray, formerly vice president of the National Farmers Union and now chair of the Land Stewardship Project, is quoted by Joe Paddock (in *Soil and Survival*):

> The singular cause of the problems of agriculture is overproduction. It is bankrupting farms. It is causing a devastating depletion of top-soil and underground water. It is endangering the entire economy. . . . We cannot save the rural economy and we cannot save the soil and water resources unless we cut production not just a little, but a lot.

The 1985 Farm Bill was supposed to reduce production. It also included some legislation to encourage land conservation, at the urging of a broad coalition of church, environmental, and farm groups. But production cuts have not occurred. Other aspects of U.S. farm and food policy include its effects on Third-World food production, landlessness, land concentration, fair trade, and access to credit.

Weighing Policy Options

A document entitled "Criteria for Assessing Policy Options for Responding to the U.S. Farm Crisis" is a useful tool for conferences, congregations, and individuals concerned about the farm crisis. It represents the combined thinking of a broad spectrum of Christian farmers and food and agricultural policy advocates. The statement provides guidelines for Christians to use for evaluating national and international equitable food and agricultural policy.

This document is from a March 1987 Consultation on Food and Agricultural Policy sponsored by Interfaith Action for Economic Justice, an ecumenical church organization based in Washington, D.C. Among other things, it recommends these criteria:

• Commodity programs that provide an equitable return on labor and management, and a supply management program that matches supply and demand as well as helps small- and medium-sized owner-operated farms.

• Farm credit at interest rates favoring minority-owned and family-sized operations, with strong protection of borrowers' rights.

• Priority access by previous owners, minorities, and new-entry farmers to inventoried land held by the government, private banks, and insurance companies.

• Land stewardship, conservation of resources, and increased incentives for regenerative agriculture.

• Reduction of crop-acreage base each time a farm is sold to a nonproducer.

• Continued modification of tax laws to strengthen moderate-sized farms.

• Government-sponsored research designed to meet the needs of appropriately scaled owner-operated and minority-owned units.

• Attention to the needs of those displaced from farms and to the increased needs of rural communities.

The document recommends that any proposed change in U.S. farm policy should assist, or at least not undermine, developing nations' efforts toward food self-reliance.

The statement also calls on Congress to commission studies to examine the role of U.S.-based transnational agribusiness with respect to food trade, food production, the achievement of food self-reliance in food-deficient countries, the debt of developing nations, and the preservation or regeneration of natural resources. It asks Congress to hold hearings on U.S. agribusiness, the U.S. food-processing sector, and implications of scientific research, especially biotechnology, on the U.S. food system.

Earthkeepers' Response

The document has no easy answers, but it can help us ask important questions and develop appropriate responses to the farm crisis.

39. Issues of the North American Farm Crisis

From 1984 a series of Faith and Farming conferences has been convened where farm families and other church people can explore the issues surrounding the farm crisis. At the fourth such conference, held at Laurelville Mennonite Church Center in Pennsylvania in 1987, Art outlined 10 farm- and food-policy issues we believe must be addressed by the churches:

1. *The continuing loss of family farms, resulting in the concentration of land ownership*

Family farms are still going out of business by the thousands. A report to the U.S. Congress from its Office of Technology Assessment estimates that half the remaining U.S. farms will be out of business by the year 2000. They claim that 72,000 farms may be lost each year until then. At the present rate of loss, minority farms (black, Hispanic, Native American) are expected to be nearly all gone by 2000.

2. *The rapid deterioration of rural communities*

It is reported that for every six farmers forced out of business, one local business is also lost. Local schools, churches, and community organizations become stressed. As local needs increase, resources decrease and the rural community deteriorates.

3. *The neglect of a proper land-stewardship ethic and/or an appropriate creation theology*

It is apparent that many Christians, including some who work the land, have neglected good land stewardship. They do not relate their work and action sufficiently to the care of creation. They have fully accepted modern industrial business and consumerism, which is often in sharp conflict with environmental ethics.

4. *The abuse of earth's natural resources*

Because so many Christians (and others) have neglected biblical environmental ethics, severe degradation is now occurring on the earth. Included in this degradation are soil erosion, water pollution, overdraft of groundwater, loss of cropland due to development and surface mining, fossil-fuel depletion, carbon-dioxide buildup (greenhouse effect), ozone depletion, rain-forest destruction, genetic erosion, and species extinction. An environmental debt of massive proportions is accumulating.

5. *The unsustainability of modern industrial agriculture*

Natural-resource abuse described above is hastened by present agricultural practices. Alternative agriculture must be adopted now before the resource base is further eroded. Sustainable agriculture renews, regenerates, and enhances the resource base—it does not destroy it.

6. *The increasing control of agriculture by petrochemical, pharmaceutical, and other industrial corporations*

Plant breeding, agricultural-chemical development, and genetic engineering are coming under control of powerful corporations. Along with plant and animal patents, a few companies may eventually control much of agriculture from seed to market. Corporate control of poultry, hogs, and cattle is also increasing. The church needs to develop guidelines for response to special patenting, genetic engineering, and corporate control in agriculture in the near future.

7. *The bankruptcy of industrial agriculture's "cheap food" policy*

Industrial agriculture is able to produce cheap food abundantly. One American farmer now is said to produce enough food for 78 persons. But American agriculture is productive at the expense of the environment. It exchanges soil, oil, and water for cheap food, causing pollution in the process. Americans do not pay farmers the real cost of food.

It takes North American Farmers nearly two calories of energy to produce one calorie of food grain. It takes Chinese wet-rice farmers only one calorie to produce 50 calories of rice. Industrial agriculture is highly productive, but energy wasteful.

8. *The failure to relate Christian faith to economic reality*

The world's economic systems do not adequately take into account the reality of God's natural ecological laws. Economic systems today do not fully recognize the constraints of nature. They operate as if there were a free lunch. Left to run rampant, our economic systems exploit people, nature, or both in the pursuit of wealth. They operate on the principles of arrogance, ignorance, and greed.

9. *The lack of church involvement with governmental farm and food policy*

There may have been a time when there was less need for governmental involvement in agriculture. That time is no more. American agriculture is part of a global system today. There are now five billion people to feed in the world. There is not a country today whose government does not regulate agriculture in some way. People and governments decide what kind of agricultural system they will have. Few churches have been sufficiently involved with government in developing an appropriate farm and food system, one that is equitable for all and at the same time sustainable.

10. *The effects of American industrial agriculture on the people of the Third World*

David and Marcia Pimentel survey this in their book *Food, Energy and Future of Society* (Niwot, Colo.: University Press of Colorado, page 137). If all the world's farms were industrialized like most American farms, the world would run out of petroleum in 11 years. Americans import about one-third of the oil and a good share of many other natural resources used in agriculture and industry. Poor countries can't compete because we use more than our fair share of the world's natural resources.

America's "cheap" foods are overproduced in pursuit of profit. These excess foods are then sold or dumped on to Third-World markets. There they undercut the local peasant producer who uses ecological means to grow his food and must earn the real costs of production. Sometimes multinational corporations go to Third-World countries, secure the best farm land, and grow crops for export. Poor local peasants must use marginal land and remain hungry.

Earthkeepers' Response

These are some of the farm- and food-policy issues that Christians ought to address. There are lots of related questions to be raised on each issue. These questions need thorough examination and testing on the basis of Christian faith. All of us, whether farmers or not, need to be involved with this. It is our hope that church leaders will take seriously the call from Laurelville's Faith and Farm Conference IV to initiate further dialogue on these important issues of North American farm and food policy.

Discussion Questions

1. The "cheap food" policy of the United States is discussed in the first article in this section. Consider the percentage of family income spent on food in various countries. Do you think it equitable that Americans spend so little? What answers do you see to this problem?

2. Cheap food is produced today at the expense of the natural environment. How can this unsustainable practice be reversed?

3. What is the overall conclusion drawn from the study described in the article on the Pentagon tax impact? What are the implications of this conclusion?

4. James Anderson, in the Pentagon article, links low farm, commodity prices with an overpriced dollar, cutting taxes, raising the military budget, and high interest rates. Discuss these factors as they relate to the loss of family farms.

5. Most of the cost of food to consumers today comes from processing, transportation, distribution, advertising, and retailing. The farmer (producer) gets little. How might this be changed?

6. How do you think the problem of overproduction of food commodities in the U.S. should be resolved? Would there be overproduction if sustainable farming practices were followed? Discuss.

7. Evaluate the items listed in "Criteria for Assessing Policy Options for Responding to the U.S. Farm Crisis." Which seem most appropriate in terms of Christian perspective?

8. Review and discuss each of the 10 farm- and food-policy issues described in the last article of this section. Prioritize and expand on each as time permits.

9. Less than 3 percent of the U.S. population is actively engaged in farming (16 percent among Mennonites). Yet food is a universal requirement for life. Who should be involved in defining and implementing a just, participatory, and sustainable farm and food policy? What is the church's role?

Resources

Bhagat, Shantilal P. *The Family Farm: Can It Be Saved?* Elgin, Ill.: The Brethren Press, 1985. Clear, concise discussion of the farm crisis by a Christian agricultural economist. Six chapters with study questions.

Common Ground. A 55-minute VHS video cassette produced for public TV (NOVA and National Audubon Society), 1987. Correlates farming and effective use of natural resources. Free loan from Land Stewardship Project, 512 W. Elm St., Stillwater, MN 55082; 612 430-2166.

"Criteria for Assessing Policy Options for Responding to the Farm Crisis." From MCC U.S. Global Education, Box M, Akron, PA 17501; 717 859-1151.

Down on the Farm: Examining Agriculture's Twin Dilemmas, Land and Profit. NOVA-produced 55-minute video cassette. Free loan from Center for Rural Affairs, Box 405, Walthill, NE 58067.

Freudenberger, C. Dean. *Food for Tomorrow?* Minneapolis: Augsburg Press, 1984. We don't have an agricultural problem in America—agriculture is the problem, says the author. One of the best summaries of worldwide food issues that we've seen.

From This Valley: On Defending the Family Farm. Produced by the Office of Interpretation, General Assembly Mission Board, Presbyterian Church USA. 1986. A 20-minute VHS video cassette outlining the history of family farming in the U.S. and the church's role in defending the family farm. Excellent introduction. For purchase from the above office at 341 Ponce De Leon Avenue, Atlanta, GA 30365.

Paddock, Joe, and others. *Soil and Survival: Land Stewardship and the Future of American Agriculture.* San Francisco: Sierra Club Books, 1986.

Platt, LaVonne Godwin, editor. *Hope for the Family Farm.* Newton,

Kans.: Faith and Life Press, 1987. Thirteen essays on the farm issue, several by Art and Jocele Meyer. The only recent book giving Anabaptist perspectives on farm issues.

Sider, Ronald J. *Rich Christians in an Age of Hunger*. Downers Grove, Ill.: InterVarsity Press, 2nd rev. ed., 1984; Dallas: Word Publishing, 3rd ed., 1990.

Agriculture and the Third World

Then the King will say:
I was hungry and you gave me something to eat,
I was thirsty and you gave me something to drink,
I was a stranger and you invited me in,
I needed clothes and you clothed me,
I was sick and you looked after me,
I was in prison and you came to visit me.
I tell you the truth,
whatever you did
for one of the least of these brothers of mine,
you did for me.
      —Matthew 25:34-36, 40

My Neighbor Is Hungry

I Was Hungry
and you fed your animals with my food

I Was Hungry
and your transnationals planted your
winter tomatoes on our best land

I Was Hungry
and you wouldn't give up your steak
from South America

I Was Hungry
but they grow tea for you where rice
might grow for my daily meal

I Was Hungry
but you turned our sugarcane and
manioc into fuel for your cars

I Was Hungry
but the waste from your factories is
poisoning the fishing grounds of the earth

I Was Hungry
but with your money you bought up my food

I Was Hungry
while my land grows exotic fruits for
your table

What Are You Afraid Of?
foregoing excessive and harmful consumption?
having to change your attitudes?
the power of the politicians?
the work involved in achieving greater
self-sufficiency?
the disapproving looks of your neighbors?

What Are You Afraid Of?
I was hungry but you gave me no food.

    —Author unknown

40. North American Agriculture and World Hunger

The Findings Committee of the Faith and Farm Conference held at Laurelville Mennonite Church Center in November 1984 made the following statement: "We are not sufficiently aware of the connection between global issues such as world hunger, world soil destruction, food costs, etc., and the way we live and farm. For example, our misuse of petroleum products in our farming practices is related to world hunger and world need."

It was clear at the conference that participants genuinely wanted to know how to be faithful in their farming practices. A deep Christian commitment was apparent. They were aware of 1 John 3:17 (TEV), "If a rich person sees his brother in need, yet closes his heart against his brother, how can he claim that he loves God?"

They recognized that the message of the good Samaritan is for us all—our neighbor is anyone in need. They knew that half the world's people live in relative poverty, a billion are malnourished, and 500 million are starving. And they were aware that some North American farmers were going broke producing more food than they can sell profitably. That made them uneasy. They wanted to know more about the global connections of their farm business.

Global Connections

Many of the relationships between world hunger and the way we live and farm in North America are obscure. One of the reasons is that most agriculture is no longer a culture but a business—agribusiness. We have separated our economic life from ethics. We still recognize the economic themes in the Bible: earth and its bountiful resources are good; there is a legitimate place for the physical world and material things; creation is good. But we separate these themes from our business practice.

The New Testament describes the "good news of salvation." Nowhere does it discuss the economic system as such. We should be aware, however, that Jesus clearly describes the consequences of economic injustice: poverty, exploitation of the poor by the rich, the perils of prosperity, the twin evils of greed and covetousness, and the dangers of wealth.

To visualize the connections between North American agriculture and world hunger, we must test our economic practices with the teachings of Jesus. When we do this, the relationships become more apparent. To understand these interactions better, we also need to look at the characteristics of both North American agriculture and world hunger.

Since World War II, North American agriculture has developed into a global agribusiness. The U.S. economy became the most powerful and most wealthy in the world following World War II. Numerous causes for this may be mentioned. Shantilal P. Bhagat, staff member for global justice with the Church of the Brethren, gives three reasons in the book *What Does It Profit?*

• No other country in the world inherited more natural wealth —rich land, minerals, energy, and climatic resources—than the U.S.

• Resourceful people who settled the land saw a need to mechanize due to an acute labor shortage. This led to a rapid expansion of the economy.

• A characteristic of U.S. capitalism is to seek continuous growth in order to survive. Once the domestic economy was well developed, the capital owners looked for expansion outside the U.S. This included the food and agriculture sector.

The U.S., its homeland unscathed by World War II, was in a

good position to expand its economy at home and abroad. The Third World became a profitable place in which to develop business. Bhagat gives these incredible profit figures for multinational businesses in 1980: in Asia, 45.2 percent; in Africa, 39.8 percent; in Latin America, 19.4 percent. In the U.S. comparable profits were only 10 percent.

Today the North American economy is dependent on the global economy. So is agribusiness. For example, two acres out of each five in the U.S. now grow crops for export.

Overconsumption by the Rich

Even though the U.S. has abundant natural resources, in our rapid economic and agricultural expansion since 1945, it has become necessary to import much from the Third World. The U.S. has less than 5 percent of the world's population today, but uses over 25 percent of the world's natural resources. We have about 50 percent of all the world's wealth. And still we desire more. Our overconsumption is further documented by these items from Ron Sider's book *Rich Christians in an Age of Hunger* (1984):

- In 1982, the 775 million people in rich countries consumed almost as much grain (428 million tons) as the 2.2 billion people (475 million tons) in the Third World.

- The United Nations reported in 1974 that livestock in the rich countries ate as much grain as did all the people in India and China.

- In 1979 and 1980, U.S. residents had diets averaging 3,624 calories per person, 138 percent of daily requirement. People in Chad had 1,808 calories each, 76 percent of daily requirement.

With our increasing wealth and the great economic inequities in the world, our help for the poor could be increasing also. But statistics show that the richer the U.S. has become, the less we have shared. In 1947 we contributed 2.79 percent of our total gross national product (GNP) to assist poor countries. In 1960 it was only 0.53 percent, and in 1988 just 0.23 percent. Out of 18 rich countries, U.S. is now eighteenth and Canada eighth in assistance to poor countries. Even then, much of the U.S. aid is in the form of military aid.

To maintain our industrial and agricultural system, we must import many strategic minerals from the Third World. Here are several U.S. imports and percentages supplied by poor countries: aluminum, 82 percent; graphite, 87 percent; and tin, 97 percent.

Rich countries consume most of the world's nonrenewable resources. Europe, North America, Russia, Japan, and Australia combined use these percentages of world supplies: petroleum, 83; natural gas, 92; nickel, 94; aluminum, 90.

Energy consumption of rich countries compared to poor ones is striking. In 1980 in kilograms of coal equivalent per person, the U.S. used 10,410; USSR, 5,595; Mexico, 1,770; Ethiopia, 29.

Steinhart and Steinhart in an article in *Science* say: "To feed the entire world with a U.S.-type food system, almost 80 percent of the world's energy expenditure would be required just for the food system." The Third World finds it difficult to compete with us for the ingredients to increase their own food production. They could not use our system of agriculture even if they wanted to.

Sometimes North American farmers are given the impression that they grow enough food to "feed the world." It is true that our farmers are the most "productive" in the world and that we are the world's leading exporter of food. One farmer in North America can feed 78 people today. But in terms of energy efficiency, North American food production is costly and not sustainable in the long term. The unpaid costs in terms of soil erosion and land and water pollution are not visible and are rarely considered. Remember that 44 percent of U.S. cropland is eroding at a rate faster than nature can rebuild it.

Though we are the world's leading food exporter, we are also third among the top importers of food, after Japan and West Germany. The United States imports 40 percent of all beef in world trade. Over two-thirds of our imports come from the Third World. We generally import more food from developing nations than we sell or give to them.

Selfish Aid

Food exported on an aid basis is usually not a gift but sold on long-term low-interest financing. Such food aid constitutes only about 5 percent of our commercial exports. Most of our agricultural exports (56 percent) go to industrialized countries like Japan, Netherlands, and West Germany. It might better be said that the role of the U.S. in the world is not feeding the hungry but selling to the rich!

Sometimes our food surpluses are dumped on poor countries. This subsidized food depresses local markets and contributes to the poverty of the farmers there.

Our food-marketing industry has on occasion worked to modify the food habits of people in the Third World, making them dependent upon our food imports. This also discourages local, self-reliant food production.

U.S. food aid is sometimes used as a political tool to force compliance with political or military objectives. Lester R. Brown of Worldwatch Institute (Paper 85) says: "We talk about the OPEC oil cartel. But the U.S. and Canada have virtual monopolistic control of the world's exportable grain supplies. In fact, the percentage of all international grain exports controlled by North America is much higher than the percent of oil exports controlled by OPEC." This kind of control usually works to the disadvantage of the poor countries.

Third-World governments, particularly in Africa, see the need to develop their domestic food production for their own political security. They have looked to Western agriculture as a model of success, using the latest technology. Foreign aid agencies will lend money for such technology in preference to supporting policies designed to help peasants in small, less-spectacular ways. Agribusiness is ready, willing, and eager to advise on large-scale technical agriculture—for a profit.

The adoption of large-scale schemes and the encouragement and financial guarantees offered by the aid agencies brings the multinational agribusinesses into the domestic food sector of the Third World. Contracts arranged by aid agencies such as U.S. Aid for International Development (USAID) or the World Bank also have the advantage of being largely immune from recessions and national cutbacks. Aid agencies effectively guarantee payments and therefore eliminate the financial risks to agribusiness. These companies benefit enormously from such aid.

Roughly 75 percent of USAID assistance funds are actually spent in the U.S. Every dollar that American taxpayers pay into the World Bank generates about $10 in procurement contracts for U.S. companies. The Third-World poor benefit little.

The kind of large-scale, energy-intensive Western agriculture used by multinationals in the Third World does not really address the underlying problems of rural hunger and poverty. Sider notes that one billion people will enter the job market between 1970 and 2000. "A successful long-term food policy must focus on things like creating jobs and redistributing resources (including skills and lands) so that people can grow or buy the food they need."

Multinational agribusinesses are not prepared to do this. In fact, they do the opposite. They buy up the best land for large-scale export cropping. Their technology eliminates rather than creates needed local employment. Exporting our agribusiness or our surplus food is not an appropriate way to solve the world hunger problem. Every country in the world has the capacity to feed itself. We should help to remove the obstacles that interfere with poor people taking control of their own food production.

Doing Ecojustice

William Gibson, social ethics professor at Cornell University, identifies the key problem. What's needed, he claims, is ecojustice (economic and ecological equity; see chapter 4, above): "The overriding issue . . . in the last two decades of this century is whether full employment can be combined with ecological responsibility." In other words, people must be able to grow their food in an ecologically sustainable way or have meaningful work which gives them the ability to buy their food or both.

Many sources indicate that the primary cause of world hunger is economic poverty. Poor people do not have access to needed resources to grow or buy food. We have already seen ways that our industrialized agricultural economy helps to perpetuate poverty. How is this related to overpopulation?

Historically, Third-World populations have been in equilibrium (stable). As science and health technology was introduced to the underdeveloped countries, life spans increased and birth rates remained constant. The result was a population explosion. Competition for local food and space led to increasing hunger and poverty. Food production improvements did not keep up with the population increase.

Because of the new vulnerability on the part of the poor, they tended to have larger families for their own security. Thus occurred a vicious cycle of poverty, overpopulation, hunger, then more poverty. Health improvements without accompanying integrated development programs, including increased food production and job creation, perpetuate the poverty-hunger cycle and overpopulation. Poverty therefore tends to lead to overpopulation, not the reverse. Adequate food production and employment are the two important factors in human population stabilization. North American agriculture as practiced today helps to perpetuate the hunger-overpopulation cycle.

Earthkeepers' Response

As one understands more fully the connections between North American agriculture and hunger, appropriate responses emerge:

• Agriculture must again become a way of life (a culture). In a finite natural world, it cannot continue in its present unsustainable direction.

• We need to put biblical ethics at the foundation of our farming practices. No other measure is right or will bring justice. No other way will work in the long run.

• Farming must change from a growth-economics system to one that is stable, regenerative, and sustainable. It must respect the natural laws of energy and environment.

• Agricultural technology in the First World should scale down while in the Third World it should scale up. Every country needs to be encouraged to become self-reliant in food production. For this to happen, sharing of wealth, power, and expertise must be done on an international level.

• Modest family farms must be protected. They are more able and more likely to follow a type of agriculture that is sustainable. Governments should be encouraged to set farm policy that assures this.

- Let the 97.6 percent of the population not farming become informed on food and agriculture issues. They must be involved and support government policies that will work toward a more sustainable type of agriculture. Part-time, small-scale farming should be an option for this group.

- Our governments must be encouraged to share more of our food surpluses with any country in need. This food aid should be used carefully and only until such time as the local people can recover their own adequate food-production system.

- Mission boards and development agencies need to increase their sharing of power, wealth, and expertise in integrated development programs with the people of the Third World. Hunger problems can be resolved only as more genuinely compassionate sharing is done by those who have. The inequities between First- and Third-World people have developed over a long time from many past injustices. Informed, caring people can act to remove these inequities. Change will take time. Sensitive Christians will want to see the process begun and moving in the right direction. The time for that is now.

Discussion Questions

1. What do you understand to be the difference between agriculture and agribusiness?

2. Review Bhagat's reasons for U.S. agriculture's production increases since World War II. Do you agree or not? Why?

3. To what extent do you agree that overconsumption of natural resources by the West affects food production in the Third World?

4. List and discuss ways in which the export of U.S. food to the Third World hampers food self-sufficiency in the receiving nation.

5. Review the analysis of poverty and overpopulation as it relates to agriculture. To what extent do you agree with the analysis?

6. Discuss each of the proposed responses to the issues in this chapter. With which do you agree? Disagree? What is your reaction to the issues raised?

7. To what extent is the international debt crisis responsible for

the farm crisis? Discuss this in terms of commodity exports and additional production by Third-World countries.

8. All producers and consumers increasingly feel the results of living in a global economy. How do you recommend that North American agriculture adapt and respond to that situation?

Resources

Brown, Lester R. *The Changing World Food Prospect: The Nineties and Beyond*. Worldwatch Paper 85, October 1988. Good analysis of world food needs and implications. From Worldwatch Institute, 1776 Mass. Ave. NW, Washington, DC 20036.

Business of Hunger. Franciscan Communications, 1984. A 28-minute 16mm film describing cash cropping, multinationals, and world trade in agriculture. Well done, provocative. For free loan from MCC, Akron, PA 17501.

Consortium for International Cooperation in Higher Education. *Solving World Hunger: The U.S. Stake*. P.O. Box 27, Cabin John, MD 20818: Seven Locks Press, 1986. Excellent source on secular view of why Third-World agriculture is important. Part I, "An Overview: Interdependence and Development," is especially pertinent.

Freudenberger, C. Dean. *Food for Tomorrow*. Minneapolis: Augsburg Press, 1984. Chapters 7-8.

Freudenberger, C. Dean. *Global Dustbowl*. Minneapolis: Augsburg Press, 1990. Describes the need for a new sustainable agriculture.

Kline, David. *Great Possessions: An Amish Farmer's Journal*. Berkeley, Calif.: North Point Press, 1990. Joyful living in harmony with nature.

Manmade Famine. A 55-minute VHS video cassette, produced by *The New Internationalist*, 1986. Good information on how government and international aid policies affect Third-World agriculture and hunger. Free loan from MCC, Akron, PA 17501.

Platt, LaVonne Godwin, editor. *Hope for the Family Farm*. Newton, Kans.: Faith and Life Press, 1987. Chapters 9 and 11.

Sider, Ronald J. *Rich Christians in an Age of Hunger*. Downers Grove, Ill., InterVarsity Press, 2nd. rev. ed., 1984; Dallas: Word Publishing, 3rd. ed., 1990.

Wolf, Edward C. *Beyond the Green Revolution: New Approaches for Third World Agriculture*. Worldwatch Paper 73, October 1986. Offers new ways to develop more equity in world agriculture.

Epilogue—Signs of Hope

The summer of 1988 saw a widespread shortage of rain in the Midwest along with temperatures soaring to 100 degrees Fahrenheit. Pastures turned brown in June. Livestock was fed hay stored for winter use. Old timers could not remember a year when high temperatures and dry weather hit so early in the growing season. There was talk of another dust bowl such as that of the '30s.

Scientists searched for answers to this sudden change in weather patterns. Was it cyclical? Was it a result of the greenhouse effect? Had the day of reckoning arrived? Did our use of fossil fuel, cutting of forests, and overuse of the earth's resources contribute to the drought conditions of summer 1988?

Some authorities suggest that conservation practices will not implement a reversal of the greenhouse effect for at least a generation. Have we indeed borrowed our children's inheritance of adequate water and soil and deprived us all? Whether or not the hot, dry weather was due to the greenhouse effect, there are mounting calls to change our way of living so that we consume less fossil fuel. Today we have the technical know-how for more responsible care of the environment, but we seem to lack the moral and political will to effect change.

The creeping Sahel in Africa, devastated lands in Vietnam, and overcropped hillsides of Central America all point to human-caused degradation of the earth. A natural catastrophe such as drought highlights the devastation caused by inappropriate agricultural and industrial practices. What then are we to do?

Many people already are intentionally living in ways that use less of the world's finite resources so that generations to come will still have a fair share. They live simply so that others may simply live. Let us look at some of these examples of care for the environment that we see as signs of hope.

Planting Trees in Haiti

On a recent visit to the tiny country of Haiti in the Caribbean, we observed eroded, denuded hillsides. This island nation, once covered with trees, now has less than 3 percent forested land. Dust and heat were oppressive. Formerly flowing mountain streams were beds of rocks. We passed a reservoir in the mountains that is the source of hydropower for much of the country. Silt eroding from the hillsides is filling it, so that only constant dredging keeps it usable.

But, amid the degradation and poverty in Haiti, we saw a project sponsored by the Pan American Development Foundation (PADF). Arlin Hunsberger, a former MCC worker, currently heads this project. Nationwide about 30 million trees have been planted in the past five years. About half of them survive the trying climate and grazing goats. The present aim is to plant 10 million trees annually. While this does not keep up with the 35 to 40 million cut yearly, it is a good start.

Hunsberger sees the need for an integrated program of education regarding use of trees and planting efforts. Even though people and financial resources are now available for this work, he predicts that it will take 50 years to turn the situation around.

Forming Cooperative Groups

Another project in the north of Haiti is part of a 10-year community-development endeavor by MCC in Mombin Crochu. This village and the surrounding rural area are isolated from the rest of the country because of poor mountain roads. It is difficult to bring in supplies and transport products out for sale. The people are working at becoming more self-sufficient so that they can raise their own food for an adequate diet. Improved infrastructure is slowly coming into the area.

MCC, working with local churches and community groups, is enabling people to make the most of local resources. These local cooperative groups see the value of working together to bring about change. Animation teams are trained to teach local agriculture and health workers. There is a swell of grassroots effort and interest. People are becoming more productive as they learn how to solve problems and work together.

After trying various methods for a number of years, MCC workers modeled a program to improve yield of local food crops. Its four main points are: eliminating the custom of burning residue to clear gardens; practicing deeper soil tillage that turns all organic matter under and improves water filtration and the water holding capacity of soil during dry spells; using contour barriers made of soil, plants, or rocks to stop soil erosion; and using dry chemical fertilizer and/or green manure crops to improve soil fertility (Fred Musser in *The Hoe*, Spring 1987).

The first year of this project, it was difficult to find enough persons interested. MCC workers modeled the program in their own vegetable gardens. The second year, after local people saw results, interest and participation grew. The third year saw more persons wanting to participate than could be included. One trained animator is so sure of the success of the program that he is giving his time without pay. Grant money had paid animation team members for time in training and teaching. It is hoped that funds will again be available.

The cooperative groups are beginning to assume leadership roles in their community activities. Many helped register voters and are taking an interest in activities of their community.

Reviving Lake Erie

Not all examples of attempts to be stewards of the creation are overseas. The Cuyahoga River, flowing into Lake Erie at Cleveland, Ohio, was once dubbed "the river on fire." An oil spill from a tanker and other pollution in the river burned for several days on the river's surface. Factories along the river regularly dumped in wastes which drained into the lake. With sewage from this most populous county in Ohio also finding its way into the lake, many fish died, poisoned by the water. Commercial and pleasure fishing in populous areas stopped. The fish that survived were full of chemicals and not safe to eat. Most of the swimming beaches were so contaminated that they were closed.

Then environmentalists and government regulations worked together to clean up the lake, which has begun to come back. The waters are clearer, although tests still show high bacterial counts. Fish again inhabit parts of the lake, although we are cautioned to eat lake fish only once a month because of the residue of heavy metals found in the flesh of the fish.

Individual Efforts

Many of our friends have taken a special interest in trees. Gordon Hunsberger, St. Jacobs, Ontario, tells us that Ross Shantz, a Mennonite farmer in the St. Agatha area of Ontario, has recently been reforesting the corners of his farm. He plants some trees every year and now has at least five acres of white pine, oak, cherry, walnut, ash, and maple trees. He plants not so much for his benefit as for that of future generations.

Shantz's interest in planting trees is connected to efforts of MCC Ontario to work at agricultural concerns, including tree planting. At community auction sales to raise funds for MCC relief work, the MCC Ontario Agricultural Concerns Committee sold tree seedlings provided by Shantz.

Increased green plants use more of the CO_2 given off by use of fossil fuel, decreasing the buildup that leads to the greenhouse effect. Yet these efforts are not enough in themselves to reverse the trend. Individually and corporately, we must also curtail the use of resources.

Many people limit their use of items made from plastic, a petroleum derivative. With encouragement by consumers and regulations by government, more responsible methods for use and disposal of plastics can become available.

Styrofoam products have special problems since their manufacture releases chlorofluorocarbons (CFCs) into the atmosphere, depleting the ozone layer needed to filter the sun's ultraviolet rays. Some manufacturers claim their product does not release CFCs. If so, they still create waste problems because they release toxic compounds when burned, are bulky for landfills, and last for centuries without chemically breaking down.

Many of our acquaintances will not purchase Styrofoam articles. Instead, they use paper products or washable dishes. Others limit their patronage of fast-food restaurants, users of large quantities of Styrofoam. Plastics are difficult to dispose of and are made from nonrenewable petrochemicals. To remind ourselves of these problems, we regularly save plastic forks and spoons when they are used, carrying them home in a napkin. This frequently is a conversation starter concerning use of nonrenewable resources.

Residents of the Deer Spring Partners Land Trust in Ohio attempt to limit their use of packaging materials. To recycle those materials that do accumulate, they have built a small shed housing containers for newspaper, aluminum, iron, other metals, glass, and household plastics. Neighbors who are not members of the partnership take advantage of this nearby collection center. State funds provide a facility in the county seat that pays nominal amounts for the reusable materials.

Individual efforts can make a difference. When George Fast of Ontario got concerned about environmental issues, he took his concern to the annual meeting of MCC Ontario. He and others in the Kitchener area organized a paper-recycling drive that spread congregation to congregation. As the idea caught on, a waste-disposal company saw the economic opportunities of recycling and introduced blue boxes for recyclable materials. Soon they appeared on streets throughout the city of Kitchener. The word spread to other municipalities, and soon Kitchener became known as the recycling capital of Canada.

Since our home is located in a wooded area, trees provide a cool site in summer. Even during the prolonged heat of summer, air conditioning is not needed. Orientation to the sun provides supplemental heat in winter. Unfortunately, unless home owners insist, few builders use the natural assistance of the environment for heating and cooling.

Gordon and Tillie Hunsberger built an energy-efficient house in 1981 in Ontario. It has a southern exposure, outside walls with six-inch insulation batts plus one-inch styrofoam sheeting, and plenty of attic insulation. It is heated by an electric furnace and a wood stove. Gordon writes, "We use about two cords of wood per season. The total electric bill for 1988 was $800—that includes lighting, cooking, water heater, and clothes dryer as well as heat."

"Builders could do much more to conserve energy when constructing houses," Gordon says, "Unfortunately many do not unless it is asked for." Fortunately, more and more people are designing their own houses to be more energy efficient. This is a hopeful sign.

Recently we visited an earth-sheltered home in southern Ohio. The owners had planned and built it themselves. It was economical to construct, used little fuel to heat, and was cool in the summer. We found this unconventional style of architecture functional and attractive.

United Action

Such organizations as the Ohio Ecological Food and Farm Association (OEFFA) encourage farmers to use fewer pesticides. OEFFA helps find markets for pesticide-free farm produce. Members have concluded that with lower inputs their profits are equal to or better than high-input farming. Most important, they are not polluting the products, farm workers, and the environment with unnecessary chemicals. Conscientious farmers have for years monitored use of pesticides.

To share common concerns, individual Mennonites are joining other Christians in groups, such as the North American Conference on Christianity and Ecology. Area groups in Kansas, Illinois, Iowa, Pennsylvania, Nebraska, and Ontario have planned faith-and-farm conferences and seminars to address such issues as waste disposal, water supply, and chemical use.

Christians would do well to band together as they address these issues. These are moral problems that need more than individual efforts and cannot be left to the government alone. Christians and the church should be in the forefront of these issues that deal so directly with God's creation.

We believe that individuals who know how lifestyles and activities affect the environment will make right choices. We hope that public policy will enable everyone to reap the benefits of careful use of the environment by limiting use of natural resources and by providing funds to research and implement alternative energy sources. We need both a concerned citizenry and a government sensitive to needs of individuals and the total group. A fully informed populace—and church—will more likely practice faithful stewardship and advocate legislation and opportunities for change.

I dare not ask what would I do if I owned Dole or Peabody Coal Company, but I need to ask, "How do I get my food?" and "How do I heat my house?" I must begin where I am.

The intent of this book is to present environmental conditions as we see them from our study and experience. We look at the facts, we look at the impact of government policies, and we look at measures promoted by environmentalists. For us that is necessary, but it is not enough. We approach our relationship with the environment as a part of our everyday Christian life. We want to add a moral consideration to our efforts. That includes respect for all parts of the creation and a oneness with the Creator.

We stand with others in the Christian community who express similar concerns. With them, we attempt to live truly as cocreators with God in our world, the world God created "in the beginning." This Creator God has commissioned us all to be earthkeepers. We seek to serve the purposes which God embedded in creation, revealed in Scripture, and continually clarifies in the midst of his people. May God's will be fulfilled on earth as it is in heaven.

For Further Study

Austin, Richard Cartwright. Environmental theology set, making a comprehensive, systematic Christian statement. Published at Louisville by Westminister/John Knox Press: *Baptized into the Wilderness: a Christian Perspective on John Muir,* 1987. *Beauty of the Land: Awakening the Senses,* 1988. *Hope for the Land: Nature in the Bible,* 1988. *Reclaiming America: Restoring Nature to Culture,* 1990.

Berardi, Gigi M., editor. *World Food, Population, and Development.* New Jersey: Rowman and Allansheld, 1985.

Brown, Lester R. *Building a Sustainable Society.* New York: W. W. Norton, 1981.

Brown, Lester R., editor. *State of the World 1990.* New York: W. W. Norton, 1990. Also issued for each year, 1985-89.

Caplan, Ruth, and others. *Our Earth—Ourselves: The Action Oriented Guide to Help You Protect and Preserve Our Environment.* New York, Dell Books, 1990.

Carmody, John. *Ecology and Religion.* Ramsey, N.J.: Paulist, 1983.

Cesaretti, C.A., and Stephen Commins, editors. *Let the Earth Bless the Lord.* New York: Harper & Row, 1981. A study guide.

Durrell, Lee. *State of the Ark: An Atlas of Conservation in Action.* London: Gaia Books, and Garden City, N.Y.: Doubleday, 1986. Researched by the International Union for Conservation of Nature and Natural Resources (IUCN).

Evans, Bernard F., and Gregory D. Cusack, editors. *Theology of the Land.* Collegeville, Minn.: The Liturgical Press, 1987.

Freudenberger, C. Dean. *Food for Tomorrow?* Minneapolis: Augsburg Press, 1984.

Friesen, Duane K. *Christian Peacemaking and International Conflict.* Scottdale, Pa.: Herald Press, 1986.

Gever, John, et al. *Beyond Oil—The Threat to Food and Fuel in the Coming Decades.* New York: Ballinger Publishing Co., 1986.

Global Ecology Handbook, The: What You Can Do About the Environment. Boston: Beacon Press, 1990. A comprehensive guide to the issues, with practical suggestions.

Granberg-Michaelson, Wesley. *Ecology and Life: Accepting Our Environmental Responsibility.* Waco, Tex.: Word, 1988.

Granberg-Michaelson, Wesley, editor. *Tending the Garden: Essays on the Gospel and the Earth.* Grand Rapids, Mich: Eerdmans, 1987.

Granberg-Michaelson, Wesley. *A Worldly Spirituality: The Call to Take Care of the Earth.* New York: Harper and Row, 1984.

Hallman, David G. *Caring for Creation.* Winfield B.C., and Oroville, Wash.: Woodlake Books, Inc., 1990.

Hessel, Dieter T., editor. *For Creation's Sake—Preaching, Ecology, and Justice.* Philadelphia: Geneva Press, 1985.

Kaufman, Milo. *Stewards of God.* Scottdale, Pa.: Herald Press, 1975.

King, Jonathan. *Troubled Water.* Emmaus, Pa.: Rodale Press, 1985.

Kreider, Carl. *The Rich and the Poor—A Christian Perspective on Global Economics.* Scottdale, Pa.: Herald Press, 1986.

Lappe, Frances M., and Joseph Collins. *World Hunger: Twelve Myths.* New York: Grove Press, 1986.

McCormick, John. *Acid Earth—The Global Threat of Acid Pollution.* Published by the International Institute for Environment and Development, 1985. Available from Earthscan, 1717 Mass. Ave. NW, Suite 302, Washington, DC 20036.

Myers, Norman, editor. *Gaia: An Atlas of Planet Management.* London: Pan Books, and New York: Anchor-Doubleday, 1984.

Naar, Jon. *Design for a Liveable Planet: How You Can Help Clean Up the Environment.* New York: Harper and Row, 1990. Includes helpful diagrams and tables.

National Geographic Magazine. December 1988. Entire issue is devoted to ecological issues.

Only One Earth. United Nations Environmental Program. DC2-803 United Nations, New York, NY 10017. Presents "earth facts" and chart, "Home Personal Action Guide."

Paddock, Joe, Nancy Paddock, and Carol Bly. *Soil and Survival: Land Stewardship and the Future of American Agriculture*. San Francisco: Sierra Club Books, 1986.

Platt, LaVonne Godwin, editor. *Hope for the Family Farm*. Newton, Kan.: Faith and Life Press, 1987.

Repetto, Robert, editor. *The Global Possible: Resources, Development, and the New Century*. New Haven: Yale University Press, 1985. A World Resources Institute Book.

Rifkin, Jeremy. *Declaration of a Heretic*. Boston: Routledge and Kegan Hall, 1985. Rifkin is a critic of nuclear technology and genetic engineering. He explains what he opposes and why, then describes the alternative view behind his own vision.

Rifkin, Jeremy, ed. *The Green Lifestyle Handbook: 1001 Ways You Can Heal the Earth*. New York: Henry Holt and Co., 1990. Handles issues and suggests responses.

Schlabach, Gerald W. *And Who Is My Neighbor?* Scottdale, Pa.: Herald Press, 1990.

Schumacher, E.F. *Small Is Beautiful: Economics As If People Mattered*. New York: Harper and Row, 1973.

Sider, Ronald J. *Rich Christians in an Age of Hunger*. Downers Grove, Ill.: InterVarsity Press, 2nd rev. ed., 1984; Dallas: Word Publishing, 3rd ed., 1990.

Sivard, Ruth Leger. *World Military and Social Expenditures*. World Priorities, Inc., Leesburg, Va., 1986. Reports for other years are also available.

Squillace, Mark. *Stripmining Handbook*. Environmental Policy Institute and Friends of the Earth, Washington, D.C., 1990. A citizen's guide to using the law to fight back against ravages of mining.

Timberlake, Lloyd. *Only One Earth*. New York: Sterling, 1987.

Time Magazine. *Planet of the Year*. January 2, 1989, issue devoted to the "endangered earth."

Weir, David, and Mark Schapiro. *Circle of Poison*. San Francisco: Institute for Food and Development Policy, 1981.

World Bank. *World Development Report 1987*. The World Bank, 1818 H Street NW, Washington, DC 20433. The 10th annual report assessing development issues. Has world development indicator tables, valuable statistical sources for understanding

food, agriculture, population, trade, and other trends
worldwide.

World Bank. *World Development Report 1990*, and previous years.
The World Bank, 1818 H Street NW, Washington, DC 20433.

World Commission on Environment and Development. *Our Common Future*. New York: Oxford Press, 1987.

World Resources Institute. *World Resources 1990-91: A Guide to the Global Environment*. New York: Oxford University Press, 1990.
Editions of other years also available.

Worldwatch Magazine. Published by Worldwatch Institute, 1776
Mass. Ave. NW, Washington, DC 20036. Bimonthly magazine
specializes in ecological issues.

Worldwatch Papers. Worldwatch Institute. The institute is an
independent, nonprofit research organization created to
analyze and focus attention on global problems. Write for list of
papers in booklet form, available by individual title or annual
subscription. Sixty-five titles to date, on energy, population,
land erosion, nuclear power, forests, cropland, pollution,
photovoltics, sustainable society, etc. Especially note these
papers:

83, *Reforesting the Earth.*

86, *Environmental Refugees: A Yardstick of Hospitability.*

87, *Protecting Life on Earth: Steps to Save the Ozone Layer.*

89, *National Security: The Economic and Environmental Dimensions.*

91, *Slowing Global Warming: A Worldwide Strategy.*

92, *Poverty and the Environment.*

94, *Clearing the Air: A Global Agenda.*

96, *Swords into Plowshares: Converting to a Peace Economy.*

The Authors

Art and Jocele were born on diversified farms in Ohio, Jocele near West Liberty and Art near Creston. Their families were actively involved in Mennonite congregations. They met at Goshen (Indiana) College; in 1950 they graduated, Jocele  in home economics and Art in biology. They were married in 1951.

Jocele taught for several years before becoming a full-time homemaker. Later she did substitute teaching, taught adult-education courses, and was involved in church and community volunteer work. She served with the Women's Missionary and Service Commission of the Mennonite Church as the national vice-president for three years and president for six years.

Art continued his professional career by going to graduate school and teaching biology in the Lakewood (Cleveland area) public schools, 1958–81. During this period the family attended the newly formed Mennonite, interracial Lee Heights (Cleveland) Community Church. Art and Jocele served the church in many capacities: education, women's groups, stewardship, and choir.

In 1981 Art was able to retire from public school teaching with full benefits. He had experienced a satisfactory and productive career, and he and Jocele decided to make a change. They accepted a term with Mennonite Central Committee (MCC) and were sent immediately to Grenada.

When the program in Grenada closed a year later, they were invited to staff the newly formed MCC Development Education Office (formerly Food and Hunger Concerns). They worked full-time in the Akron, Pennsylvania, office until 1985, when they moved to Fresno, Ohio, onto land purchased in 1973. From their home they both work half-time with MCC's Global Education Office, handling the same issues and similar projects. Research, writing, editing a newsletter, traveling, and speaking for MCC continue.

The Meyers are also involved in low-input farming on their 80 acres. Much of the land is wooded. They raise strawberries and vegetables, cultivate a 50-tree orchard, and raise a few chickens and steers. By living in a passive solar house, planting trees on unreclaimed strip-mined land, growing and preserving much of their own food, they practice responsible environmental living.

Art is interested in songbird voice and field identification, gardening, writing lyrics for hymn tunes, and travel. Jocele enjoys the outdoors, reads, does sewing and needlework, likes to cook from scratch, preserves homegrown produce, and continues with church volunteer work.

The Meyers have three grown children and eight grandchildren. They are members of Lafayette Christian Fellowship, a young Mennonite church that began with persons involved in a land trust venture which the Meyers helped begin in 1980.